400 PLUS
VOLLEYBALL
DRILLS AND IDEAS

BOB BRATTON   BRAD KILB

University of Calgary

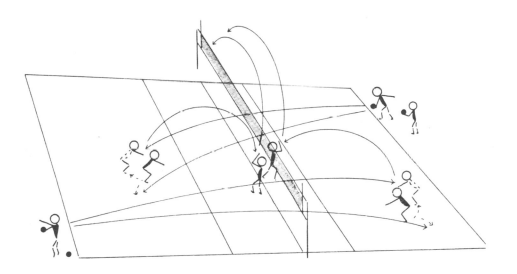

Copyright © 1985 by the Canadian Volleyball Association

Canadian Volleyball Association
1600 James Naismith Drive, Gloucester, Ontario
Canada K1B 5N4

First Printing — August 1985

ISBN 0-920412-52-1

THE AUTHORS

Dr. Bob Bratton is a Professor of Physical Education at The University of Calgary where he is a specialist in sport sociology and volleyball. He has been associated with volleyball for thirty years as a player, coach, clinician, referee, executive member, administrator, researcher and author. He has taught and coached both males and females from beginning through international levels. His study of the sport started in Chicago when he played for George Williams College and in Los Angeles while he attended U.C.L.A. His interest in learning more has taken him to France, Germany, Holland, Japan, Poland and Mexico, and he has interacted with visiting teams and coaches from the U.S.S.R., Czechoslovakia, Korea and Cuba to learn about their approaches to teaching and coaching. His first book, **Power Volleyball,** was published in 1968 and that was followed by **300 Plus Volleyball Drills and Ideas** in 1974, **Basic Volleyball Skills and Concepts with Kit Lefroy** in 1980, and **Volleyball Team Tactics and Training** in 1984.

Brad Kilb is a coach/lecturer at The University of Calgary, where he is the Head Coach of the Women's Varsity Team. Himself an international Level II FIVB Certified Coach (Japan, 1981), he is actively involved with the Canadian Coaching Certification Program as a course conductor in both the technical and theoretical levels. Recently, he has completed the revision of the Canadian Volleyball Association's Level I and II Technical Coach's and Course Conductor's Manuals. As a coach, he has directed both women's and men's teams to the National Championship Finals five times, winning sixteen conference or regional championships. Brad has been recognized as Conference and Canadian Interuniversity Coach of the Year several times. He served as Canadian National Coach (Junior Women) for four years, bringing home a NORCECA silver and a seventh place finish at the World Championships. In 1983-1984, he coached one of the top A-1 semi-professional teams in Italy. His coaching experiences have taken him to the U.S.A., Mexico, Brazil, China, Korea, Japan, Italy, Poland, Israel and Holland. His newest book, **BLUEPRINT FOR COACHING,** will come off the press later this year.

TABLE OF CONTENTS

Page

INTRODUCTION

400 Plus is a "cook book" or reference file of drills suitable for both the teacher and coach. The authors expect that the imaginative reader will use the ideas and drills presented in this text as stimulation for the creation of many more innovative solutions to specific teaching and coaching situations.

The ideas or suggestions in Part I are presented for the benefit of the student or novice teacher or coach. Many important concepts that are basic to planning and running effective classes and practices are included.

The drills have been grouped with specific objectives in mind. The teacher or coach can run through the Table of Contents, identify the appropriate objective for the lesson or practice plan, and then select the required number of drills.

The teaching progressions in Part II are samples of progressions that have proven effective in teaching basic skills to beginners. These can then be followed up with drills selected from Part III that are designed to help improve basic skills.

Part IV includes a number of intermediate and advanced drills that require a reasonable skill level before the drills can be executed effectively. Finally, drills that combine the execution of various skills in the sequence that might occur in a game are included in Part V.

LEGEND

PLAYER — STARTING POSITION

PLAYER — SUBSEQUENT POSITION

PATH OF BALL

PATH OF PLAYER

BALL

SERVE

FOREARM PASS

OVERHAND PASS

SPIKE

TIP

BLOCK

DIVE, DIG

TOSS

PART I

IDEAS FOR

PRACTICE PLANNING

INTRODUCTORY IDEAS

The ideas in this section include many that should help the teacher or coach better plan and organize practices. They should also help the student become sensitized to the many factors that are involved in planning effective classes and practices.

IDEA

Players improve by doing. Players should make as many quality contacts as possible during the time available in practice or class. To accomplish this, the teacher or coach must ensure that a ball is available for every player and that the drills or games used provide for maximum individual participation. Players improve by doing, not by standing in line waiting or listening.

IDEA

Flow from drill to drill is important to maximize ball contact. A well-planned class or practice involves the selection of appropriate drills that do flow one from the other. Many sequences have been presented in this text to assist the teacher or coach with this flow.

IDEA

Boredom interferes with learning and motivation. New drills or small changes to basic drills provide an element of novelty that serves to eliminate boredom. The variety of drills in this text should be useful. A coach can use a little imagination and add wrinkles or develop other drills.

IDEA

Challenge and competition add to the excitement of a class or practice. A number of game drills and other suggestions have been included to suggest possible ways to make classes or practices more exciting.

IDEA Drills should be appropriate to the skill level of the players. A drill that is too complex or that requires reasonable skill levels to be run effectively is not productive for lower level players. The goal of the drill should be challenging, but not so difficult as to be frustrating.

IDEA

Player-centered drills free the coach to observe, to instruct, and to take a player aside to give individual attention. The players also improve their skills in tossing, spiking or serving. At lower skill levels, however, the players often lack the control necessary for many drills to be effective.

IDEA

Coach-centered drills allow the coach to control the difficulty, intensity and tempo of the drill. The skilled coach can place the ball effectively when tossing, hitting or serving to produce specific reactions. The coach needs to develop accuracy or control with these coaching skills for the drills to be effective. The disadvantage is that the coach is very involved in running the drill and not free to offer corrections or must often stop the drill to give individual attention. The coach can get a good "workout".

IDEA

Lead-up drills place the emphasis on learning a basic movement or sequence of movements required in the final skill or game sequence. It is used in the "whole", "part", "whole" method of teaching. One might teach the approach of the spike without the ball, as an example.

IDEA

Execution-oriented drills place the emphasis on the mechanical execution of the skill. These are used when a player is first learning a skill or correcting an error. The skill is often broken down and progressions followed with feedback from the coach or partner relating to the proper hand action, arm action, leg action, etc.

IDEA

Time-oriented drills run for a specified period of time such as 30 seconds or 5 minutes. The players may attempt to contact the ball as many times as possible in the time limit, or the time limit may be used to rotate players or groups from station to station.

IDEA

Contact-oriented drills run until a player has contacted the ball 15 times or 45 times consecutively. Players then rotate stations or a new skill or drill is introduced. The number of contacts should be in multiples of fifteen, if possible, to end on the magical game-winning "15".

IDEA

Goal-oriented drills run until a specific goal is achieved involving the successful execution of the skill. Goals might include 5 serves in a row without a mistake, or 15 accurate passes to a target, or 10 blocked balls. They add interest to the practice. Set the goal to finish at 15 (i.e., for 5 serves, start at 10 and finish on 15).

IDEA

Combination drills involve more than one skill such as serving and passing, or setting, spiking and blocking. They are appropriate once the players have reasonable skill level to combine the execution of skills. At the lower skill level, however, combination drills are often wasteful because only one pass in ten is directed to the setter, or the sets are so bad that the beginning spiker finds it difficult to spike.

IDEA

Transition drills attempt to repeat as rapidly as possible the sequences that might exist in a game. The section on transition drills places a good deal of emphasis on this area. These sequences are meant to be game-like. Advanced players will spend much of their time with transition drills.

IDEA

Pressure drills place one or more players on stage in front of the rest of the group and they have to execute a skill or series of skills successfully. The drills are normally coach-centered. In addition to the pressure of executing the skill effectively, there is the additional psychological pressure of having to perform in front of an audience. This often improves concentration, as well as successful performance when physically or psychologically tired.

IDEA

Concentration drills involve a skill or sequence of skills that force the player to think about what to do next. They can be combined with goal-oriented drills to force the player or players to execute a sequence 15 times in a row without an error.

IDEA

Conditioning drills force the player to repeat the skill many times in a row until exhausted. The coach will attempt to extend the player's time limit each week. These are often combined with pressure drills or goal-oriented drills.

IDEA

Game-tactic drills are designed by the coach to help teach positions and game responsibilities as well as alternatives in execution of offensive and defensive skills.

IDEA

The coach or teacher should evaluate the effectiveness of each drill, as well as player reaction to the drill, once it is used. This can be used for future planning.

IDEA

Keep the drills simple until the basic skill is learned. Complicated drills and pressure drills can lead to bad habits and weak basic skills if they are attempted too soon. Move on to more complex drills and game-like situations as soon as the players are ready, not when the coach is ready.

IDEA

Once the basic skill is learned, add movement to the drill. Too much time spent on non-moving basic skill drills can result in static behaviour. In a game, for instance, the ball is seldom passed directly to the setter. In most instances, the setter will have to take two or more steps to set the ball.

IDEA

Young players and beginning players have some difficulty in adjusting to the speed of the ball. They require more time to move into position to play the ball properly. Allow the ball to bounce once in games and in very basic drills. This will give the child enough time to move under the ball. The use of bladders or beach balls is also helpful.

IDEA

Prepare and post a list of all of the different skills that can be learned in volleyball, including such things as underhand and roundhouse serves, back and front sets, tipping short and long, spiking line and cross-court, etc. A check-off chart posted in the gym can be an excellent motivational device and can also be used for evaluating progress and ability.

IDEA

Teach the players how to chase and collect balls rapidly. Very often time is wasted while a player saunters after a ball. If the players are always on the run, it can be part of their conditioning as well as effective in developing a hard work attitude toward practice. Also teach the player how to hand balls to the tosser, or to press the ball against the hip for the coach to take and toss or hit.

IDEA

Have the students or the players design and run a drill or sequence of drills for a class or practice. This can be an interesting challenge to the player and also place more responsibility on the player.

IDEA

Develop a club concept with two or more teams in a club. No player likes to sit on the bench, and players do not develop as rapidly sitting on the bench. A second or a third team will allow more players to get valuable playing experience and help them develop faster and allow them to fit more readily into the first team when needed. Two teams can practice together and feel part of the club. If only 5 to 6 players turn up from one team for a practice, the missing players are not as noticeable if the players from the other teams are present and practices can continue. Larger numbers can also create an atmosphere of enthusiasm and provide a larger financial base. The coach must learn how to run practices for larger numbers and recruit more assistant coaches.

IDEA

Use two courts for practicing, particularly if you have more than 10 players. This allows for more action at the net and more space to run larger drills. Running joint practices for senior and junior teams also creates a stronger feeling of support and identification.

IDEA

Teach small-sided games involving two or three players per team so that the players can play these games before the practice or class starts. These games should be vigorous and result in a good warm-up. Some suggestions are presented in the text.

IDEA

Modify the rules of the game to suit the skill level of the players. The official rules were designed for Olympic and international calibre athletes and may not always be appropriate for beginners or young players. The substitution rule can be modified or fewer players on a team such as is the case in mini-volleyball (3 per team on a badminton court) are two examples.

IDEA

Play doubles or triples volleyball with two or three players on each team. The opportunity to contact the ball is substantially increased as is the required movement. Skill and movement will improve much more rapidly. Elementary school teachers are encouraged to play mini-volleyball rather than regular six-aside volleyball.

IDEA

Use small candy prizes such as jelly beans or peanuts during practice as reinforcement each time a player successfully spikes or serves at a target.

IDEA

Use adaptations of other games involving volleyball skills as lead-up games. One example would be volley-hockey. Use the full length or the width of the gym. Use hockey goals. Players must pass the ball down the gym using either a forearm pass or an overhand pass and then spike the ball into the goal to score. To intercept the ball, the opponents must jump and tip or pass the ball. When control is lost, the opponents get to serve the ball into play from the sideline. Volley-basketball can be played the same way.

IDEA

Build your own equipment and coaching aids. Plans for a combination coaching platform and referee stand, blocking board, and target net are included. A rubber rope can also be used for conditioning or skill development.

COMBINATION REFEREE STAND
AND SPIKING PLATFORM

This plan allows the stand to be used at a height of
four feet for a referee or coach, at a height of three
feet or at a height of two feet. Numbers are painted
on white plastic and bolted to the metal frame.

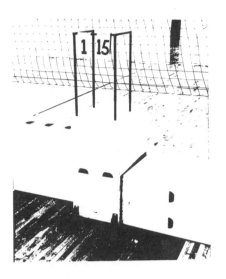

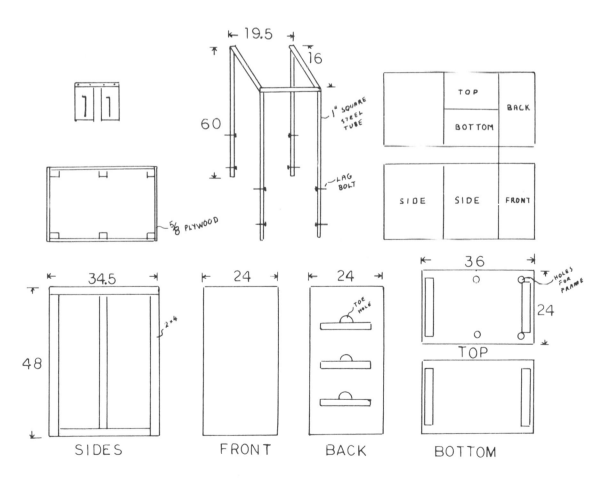

BLOCKING BOARDS

Plan A — Wood is easy to construct. Two 12 foot 2 x 4's are bolted to the sides of a 30" x 36" sheet of inch plywood. Two 1" x 4" boards 23" long are screwed to the plywood at the top and bottom between the 2 x 4 support posts for support. A foam or rubber pad is taped to the front of the plywood sheet. Holes are drilled at six inch intervals at the top of the 2 x 4 posts to allow the blocking board to be raised or lowered for men's or women's heights.

Plan B — Metal is more difficult to construct. A frame 30" x 36" is made from 1 inch steel pipe. The corners can be welded, or threaded and joined with right angle threaded connectors. At 3 inch intervals, holes are drilled at right angles through the frame. Strong nylon twine will later be woven through these holes. A slightly larger diameter pipe is welded to the middle of the top and bottom frame to allow the 10 feet long 1 inch support post to slide through. A hole is drilled through the pipe and three holes are drilled through the support pipe. A bolt or pin fits through the holes in the two pipes to fix the board at the desired height. The nylon twine is then threaded and woven through the frame and tightened to the desired tension. If possible, nylon or plastic inserts should be used in the holes to reduce friction on the twine. A roller can be attached to the bottom of the support post for ease of adjustment. A handle could also be welded to the support post to make it easier to hold.

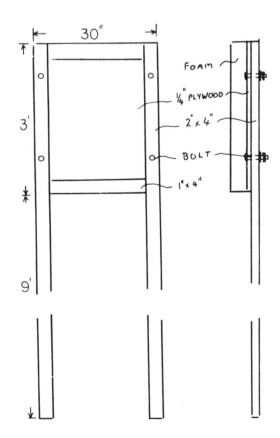

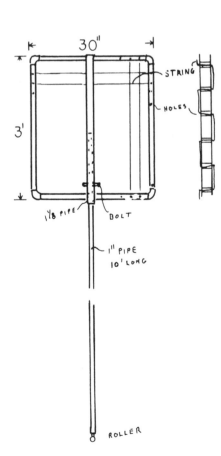

TARGET NET

A frame 3 feet x 3 feet is made from either 3/4 inch copper tubing with a wood dowel inserted to add ridigity, or from plastic tubing. Both are readily available from plumbing supply stores. A T large enough to slide over the tubing used in the frame is put on one side before the frame is assembled. The support post will be attached to this T and the T will allow for easier storage as well as the ability to tilt the target. The support post will be made of two pieces of different diameters such that one can slide inside the other, with one piece either inside or outside. One hole is drilled through one piece and several holes are drilled in the other piece to allow the frame to be adjusted to varying heights by inserting a pin or bolt through the appropriate hole. A net is attached to the frame, preferably with an open bottom and at least 5 feet long. A rope is tied around the bottom to close the net completely or to leave an opening for balls to drop through into a collection basket below. The frame is attached to the top of the net by rope or a strap. The frame can also be attached to the bottom of the net and used as a ball basket for tossing drills.

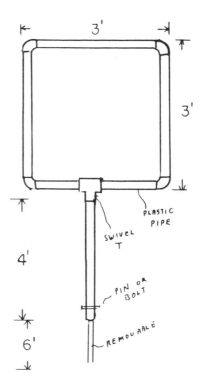

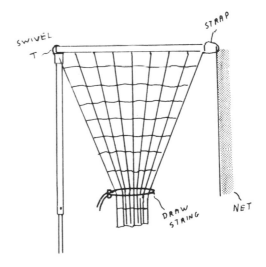

NOTES

PART II

TEACHING PROGRESSIONS

FOR BEGINNERS

OBJECTIVE
To teach the underhand serve

DRILL 1
UNDERHAND SERVE, 1 PLAYER, 1 BALL

The player holds the ball in front with the non-serving hand, rocks backward and forward without making contact with the ball. The objective is to learn to shift the weight from foot to foot and create the momentum beginners require.

DRILL 2
UNDERHAND SERVE, 1 PLAYER, 1 BALL, WALL

The player stands about 2 metres away from and facing a wall, rocks forward and backward 2 or 3 times and then serves the ball to the wall. Catch the ball and repeat.

DRILL 3
UNDERHAND SERVE, 1 PLAYER, 1 BALL, WALL

The player stands about 3 metres away from and facing a wall. Rock and serve to a spot on the wall. Catch the ball and repeat. Gradually move further away from the wall.

DRILL 4
UNDERHAND SERVE, 2 PLAYERS, 1 BALL

Two players start about 6 metres apart and serve back and forth so that the ball drops to the partner's upstretched hands. Gradually move further apart.

DRILL 5
UNDERHAND SERVE, 2 PLAYERS,
1 BALL, NET

Two players start just behind the attack lines on each side of the net and serve back and forth over the net. Concentrate on serving accurately to your partner. Gradually move further apart.

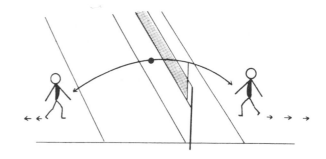

DRILL 6
UNDERHAND SERVE, 2 PLAYERS,
1 BALL, NET

One player stands about 3 metres back from the net and the other player serves accurately to the first player. The first player catches the serve, moves back and then serves to the original server who has moved into court to become a target. Gradually have the target move further back from the net and serve longer.

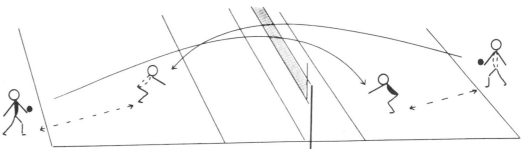

OBJECTIVE
To teach the sidearm serve

DRILL 7
SIDEARM SERVE, 1 PLAYER, 1 BALL

The player stands and holds the ball out in front of the face with the non-serving hand, twists or rotates on the wind up and rotates back without making contact with the ball. The objective is to teach the body rotation to assist with momentum.

DRILL 8
SIDEARM SERVE, 1 PLAYER, 1 BALL,
NET

The player stands about 1 metre away from the net, rotates or winds up twice and then serves the ball into the net. Catch the ball and repeat.

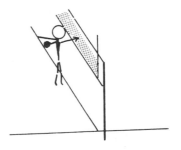

DRILL 9
SIDEARM SERVE, 1 PLAYER, 1 BALL, WALL

The player stands about 3 metres away from a wall and serves to a spot or target on the wall. Catch the ball and repeat.

DRILL 10
SIDEARM SERVE, 2 PLAYERS, 1 BALL

Two players start about 6 metres apart and serve back and forth to each other. Gradually move further apart. Concentrate on serving accurately to your partner. Try this drill by having both partners stand on a line and serve along the line.

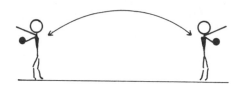

DRILL 11
SIDEARM SERVE, 2 PLAYERS, 1 BALL, NET

Two players start about mid court on each side of the net and serve back and forth to each other. Gradually move further back from the net. Serve accurately to your partner.

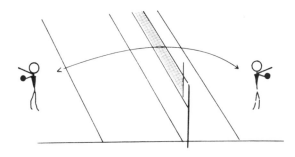

DRILL 12
SIDEARM SERVE, 2 PLAYERS, 2 BALLS, NET

One player stands in court as a target and the other serves accurately to the target. Catch the serve and roll the ball back to the server. Keep two balls going.

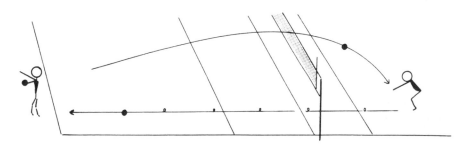

OBJECTIVE
To teach the overhand serve

DRILL 13
OVERHAND SERVE, 1 PLAYER, 1 BALL

The players tosses the ball up as if to serve and catches the ball. Repeat and learn to be very consistent with the toss or placement of the ball in the air. Do not toss too high as a high toss is more difficult to judge and to hit.

DRILL 14
OVERHAND SERVE, 1 PLAYER, 1 BALL, WALL

The player stands about 2 metres away from a wall and serves to a spot on the wall. Catch and repeat. Try to always hit the same spot on the wall.

DRILL 15
OVERHAND SERVE, 1 PLAYER, 1 BALL, WALL

The player stands about 3 metres away from a wall and serves to a target on the wall. Catch and repeat. Gradually move further away from the wall. Concentrate on the follow through action of the hand toward the target. Keep the hand up on the follow through.

DRILL 16
OVERHAND SERVE, 2 PLAYERS, 1 BALL, NET

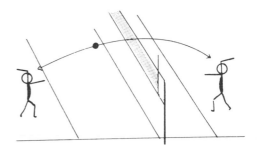

Two players start about mid court and serve back and forth over the net to each other. Gradually move further back from the net. Concentrate on serving accurately to your partner.

DRILL 17
OVERHAND SERVE, 2 PLAYERS,
1 BALL, NET

One player stands on the court as a target and the other serves. The target player passes the ball forward toward the net, steps forward and picks up the ball and then moves back to serve while the original server steps into court to become the target. Move the target around the court and serve accurately to the target.

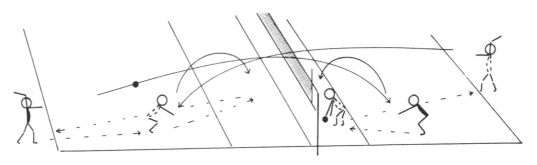

OBJECTIVE
To teach the forearm pass

DRILL 18
FOREARM PASS, 2 PLAYERS, 1 BALL

One player stands about 3 metres in front of the passer and tosses the ball from overhead directly to the passer. The passer allows the ball to bounce from the arms. Check the stance, body posture and arm position.

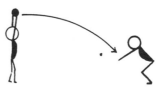

DRILL 19
FOREARM PASS, 2 PLAYERS, 1 BALL

One player stands about 3 metres in front of the passer and tosses the ball from overhead directly to the passer. The passer tries to pass the ball directly back into the upstretched hands of the tosser.

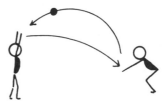

DRILL 20
FOREARM PASS, 2 PLAYERS, 1 BALL

One player stands about 3 metres in front of the passer and tosses the ball to the left or to the right of the passer. The passer must move and pass directly back to the upstretched hands of the tosser. Start with a slight movement to either side and gradually increase the movement required. Check the footwork and leg action.

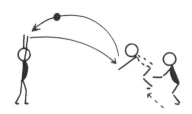

DRILL 21
FOREARM PASS, 2 PLAYERS, 1 BALL, NET

One player tosses the ball over the net and then crosses under the net and holds the hands high as a target. The passer attempts to pass directly to the target. Start by tossing accurately to the passer and then gradually force the passer to move forward or sideways to pass. The tosser can then serve the ball over the net from mid court.

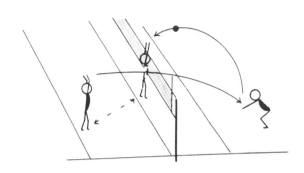

OBJECTIVE
To teach the follow through
of the body toward the target
with the forearm pass

DRILL 22
FOREARM PASS, 2 PLAYERS, 1 BALL

Two players start about 3 metres apart. (A) One player tosses a ball for the partner to pass and (B) the passer continues stepping or walking forward with the pass and touches the ball held out by the tosser.

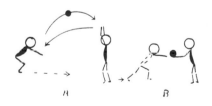

DRILL 23
FOREARM PASS, 3 PLAYERS, 1 BALL, NET

One player tosses the ball over the net to a player who passes the ball to a target player standing close to the net. The passer continues moving forward and touches the target player.

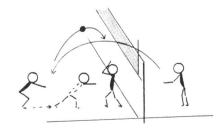

DRILL 24
FOREARM PASS, 4 PLAYERS, 1 BALL, RUBBER ROPE

Two players hold the rope at waist height or slightly lower. The passer starts about 1 metre away from the rope. The tosser throws a ball over the rope and the passer follows through with the pass by stepping forward and contacting the rope with the forearms.

OBJECTIVE
To teach the overhand pass

DRILL 25
OVERHAND PASS, 1 PLAYER, 1 BALL, FLOOR

The player kneels on one knee with the ball on the floor. Place the hands, with fingers spread, on top of the ball and press down to force the wrists back (hyper-extension). Now pick up the ball and move it above and close to the forehead. Repeat and check to see that the hands are in the proper position.

DRILL 26
OVERHAND PASS, 1 PLAYER, 1 BALL, FLOOR

The player kneels on one knee with the ball on the floor, bends forward, places the hands on top and sides of the ball, raises the ball 30 cm off the floor, bounces the ball on the floor and catches the ball with the hands and wrists in the proper position. Repeat and check proper hand and wrist position. Now speed up the action until the ball is not being caught. Emphasize the wrist action.

DRILL 27
OVERHAND PASS, 1 PLAYER, 1 BALL, FLOOR

The player bends at the waist and passes the ball to the floor. Catch the ball and repeat. Pass several times continuously and catch. Check the hand and wrist position, and action.

DRILL 28
OVERHAND PASS, 1 PLAYER, 1 BALL

The player throws the ball up and catches it above the forehead with the wrists bent back and hands in the proper position (thumbs back, fingers spread) directly above the forehead. Once the hands are in the proper position to catch the ball, the player should toss the ball up, pass it and then catch it. Repeat and check position.

DRILL 29
OVERHAND PASS, 1 PLAYER, 1 BALL, WALL

The player stands 2 metres away from a wall and throws the ball against the wall about 3 to 4 metres above the floor. The player moves under the ball and catches it. Check to see that the hand and body position are correct.

DRILL 30
OVERHAND PASS, 1 PLAYER, 1 BALL, WALL

The player stands close to the ball and passes the ball against the wall continuously. If the player uses a basketball it will help force the wrists and thumbs back and also serve to strengthen the fingers and wrists. Concentrate on relaxing the wrists and follow though with the index fingers.

DRILL 31
OVERHAND PASS, 1 PLAYER, 1 BALL, WALL

The player stands 2 metres away from the wall and throws the ball against the wall to their left or right. The player moves under the ball and catches it. Check the hand and body position.

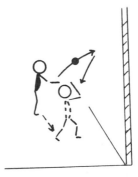

DRILL 32
OVERHAND PASS, 1 PLAYER, 1 BALL, WALL

The player stands 2 metres away from the wall and throws the ball against the wall to their left or right. The player moves under the ball and passes it high to the wall. Catch and repeat to the other side.

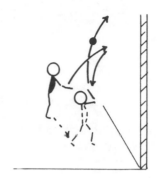

DRILL 33
OVERHAND PASS, 1 PLAYER, 1 BALL, WALL

The player stands about 2 metres away from the wall and throws the ball against the wall about 3 metres above the floor. The player moves in and crouches under the ball and catches it. Check the hand position.

DRILL 34
OVERHAND PASS, 1 PLAYER, 1 BALL, WALL

The player stands 2 metres away from a wall and throws the ball against the wall about 4 metres above the floor. The player moves under the ball and passes it to the wall. Catch the next rebound and repeat. Emphasize correct technique.

DRILL 35
OVERHAND PASS, 1 PLAYER, 1 BALL, WALL

The player starts about 2 metres away from the wall and passes the ball to various spots on the wall so that they must move or crouch to make the next pass. Do not use bad form to pass — catch the ball instead and start again. Emphasize good form.

DRILL 36
OVERHAND PASS, 2 PLAYERS, 1 BALL

The passer waits with the hands up in the proper position above the forehead. The other player tosses the ball so that it lands in the hands. The passer catches the ball. Check to see that the thumbs and wrists are back and the hands are in the proper position.

DRILL 37
OVERHAND PASS, 2 PLAYERS, 1 BALL

The passer starts with the hands up above the forehead in the proper position. The other player tosses the ball slightly to the side or in front or behind the passer. The passer moves under the ball and catches it.

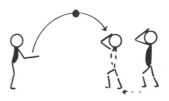

DRILL 38
OVERHAND PASS, 2 PLAYERS, 1 BALL

The passer starts with the hands up above the forehead in the proper position. The other player tosses the ball low, forcing the player to crouch under the ball and catch it.

DRILL 39
OVERHAND PASS, 2 PLAYERS, 1 BALL

The passer starts with the hands up above the forehead in the proper position. The other player tosses the ball accurately to the passer. The passer must pass the ball using the legs only. Do not try for much distance with the pass. Just let the ball drop into the pocket of the hands and bounce out using the leg action only. Check for proper hand position.

DRILL 40
OVERHAND PASS, 2 PLAYERS, 1 BALL

The passer starts with the hands above the forehead in the proper position. The other player tosses the ball slightly to one side or the other of the passer. The passer must pass the ball using mostly leg action and a slight amount of arm action — very little finger and wrist action. The purpose of this sequence is to develop the flex action of the wrists and fingers.

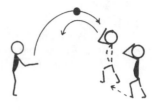

DRILL 41
OVERHAND PASS, 2 PLAYERS, 1 BALL

The passer starts with the arms down. The other player tosses the ball reasonably high and fairly close to the passer. The passer must raise the hands above the forehead early and move under the ball and pass using primarily leg action and a slight amount of arm action.

DRILL 42
OVERHAND PASS, 2 PLAYERS, 1 BALL

The passer starts with the arms down. The other player tosses the ball with a reasonable arc fairly close to the passer. The passer must raise the hands above the forehead early and move under the ball and pass using the total action of the legs, arms and wrists.

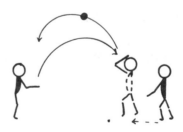

THE BEGINNING
IS THE MOST IMPORTANT
PART OF THE WORK.

OBJECTIVE
To teach the tip

DRILL 43
TIP, 1 PLAYER, 1 BALL, WALL

The player stands about 1 metre away from a wall. Toss the ball softly to the wall about 1 to 2 metres above head height and tip the rebound to the wall — no jump. Catch the ball and repeat.

DRILL 44
TIP, 1 PLAYER, 1 BALL, WALL

The player starts about 1 metre away from a wall. Toss the ball to the wall about 2 to 3 metres above head height. Jump and tip the ball to the wall. Catch the ball and repeat.

DRILL 45
TIP, 1 PLAYER, 1 BALL, WALL

The player starts about 1 metre away from a wall. Toss the ball to the wall about 2 to 3 metres above head height, jump and tip the ball and continue jumping and tipping. Catch the ball and start again when control is lost.

DRILL 46
TIP, 1 PLAYER, 1 BALL, WALL

The player starts about 1 metre away from a wall. Toss the ball to the wall about 2 to 3 metres above head height, jump and tip the ball to the wall and continue jumping and tipping with alternate hands. Catch the ball and start again when control is lost.

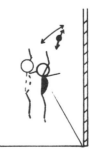

DRILL 47
TIP, 2 PLAYERS, 1 BALL, WALL

One player tosses the ball up for the other to jump and tip to the wall. Start with no approach and then add the approach to the jump. Pick a target on the wall and try to tip to the target.

DRILL 48
TIP, 2 PLAYERS, 1 BALL, NET

One player tosses the ball up for the other to jump and tip over the net. Recover the ball and exchange places. It is also possible to have the tosser cross under the net as soon as the ball is tossed and act as a target for the tipper.

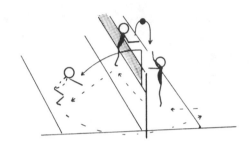

DRILL 49
TIP, 2 PLAYERS, 5 BALLS, NET, BASKET

Place the basket on the attack line on the other side of the net. One player tosses the balls for the other to jump and tip over the net into the basket. Recover the balls and exchange places. Move the position of the basket to make the tip gradually more difficult.

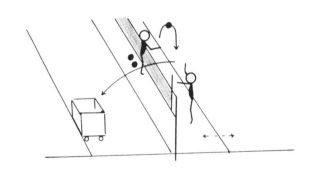

GAME 50
TIP, 2 PLAYERS, 5 BALLS, NET, BASKET

Place the basket on the other side of the net. One player tosses the balls for the other to jump and tip over the net into the basket. Recover the ball and exchange places.

Score 2 points for each ball that goes into the basket and 1 point for a ball that hits the rim.

Move the basket to a new place after each round of tips. Also tip from each of the three positions (2, 3 and 4) along the net.

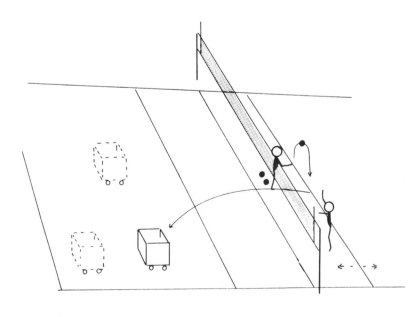

OBJECTIVE
To teach spiking arm action

DRILL 51
SPIKE ACTION, 1 PLAYER, 1 TENNIS BALL

The player throws the tennis ball at the floor. Emphasize the loose forearm action and whipping action and the snap of the wrist. Do not use the shoulder to increase the force.

DRILL 52

SPIKE ACTION, 1 PLAYER, 1 TENNIS BALL, WALL

The player stands about 3 metres away from a wall and throws the tennis ball to the floor in front of the wall. Mimic the arm lift and swing for the spike action and emphasize the whipping action of the forearm and wrist. The ball should be aimed at a point on the floor close to the wall.

DRILL 53
SPIKE ACTION, 2 PLAYERS, 1 TENNIS BALL

Two players stand about 6 metres apart and toss the tennis ball to the floor so that it bounces to the other player. Mimic the arm lift and swing for the spike action and emphasize the whipping action of the forearm and wrist. Now introduce the shoulder action and body rotation on the throw.

DRILL 54
SPIKE ACTION, 2 PLAYERS, 1 TENNIS BALL, NET, BENCH

One player stands on a bench close to the net and throws the ball down to the floor over the net. The partner catches the ball. Mimic the arm action of the spike and emphasize the whip and shoulder rotation. Do not touch the net.

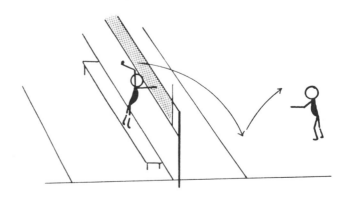

DRILL 55
SPIKE ACTION, 2 PLAYERS, 1 TENNIS BALL, NET

One player takes a one or two step approach, jumps and throws the tennis ball down to the floor over the net. Have the player now try to throw the ball to various places on the court. It may be necessary to lower the net for shorter players. The partner returns the ball.

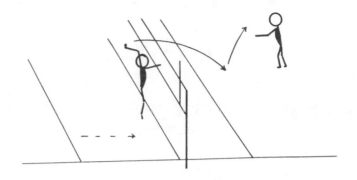

DRILL 56
SPIKE ACTION, 1 PLAYER, 1 BALL

(A) The player stands holding the ball in front of the body with the spiking hand on top of and the other hand below the ball. Lift the ball up above the head with both hands by swinging the arms. Do not release the ball. (B) Next, lift the ball above with both hands and lift the top hand off the ball and wind up. Hold the ball in the other hand. (C) Next lift the ball with both hands, lift the top hand off the ball, wind up and whip back contacting the ball while still holding it with the other hand. The ball will now be held between the two hands.

This is to simulate the lifting action of the arms on the jump as well as the wind up with the spiking arm.

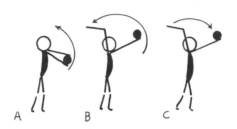

DRILL 57
SPIKE ACTION, 1 PLAYER, 1 BALL, WALL

The player stands about 3 metres from a wall and simulates the same action as in the previous drill. This time the player hits the ball and does not catch it with the other hand. Hit the ball to the floor so that it bounces from the floor to the wall and back to the player.

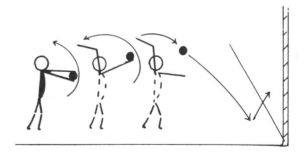

DRILL 58
SPIKE ACTION, 1 PLAYER, 1 BALL, WALL

The player stands about 4 metres from a wall and tosses the ball up in front of and above the hitting shoulder. Wind up and spike the ball to the floor close to the wall. Emphasize the reach or extension to contact the ball as well as the wrist snap and follow through action of the arm.

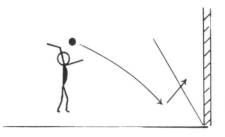

DRILL 59
SPIKE ACTION, 1 PLAYER, 1 BALL, WALL

The player starts about 4 metres from a wall and repeatedly spikes the ball to the floor emphasizing the whipping action of the arm. The player must move to the rebounding ball to be in a good position to hit it again. Catch the ball if the position is bad and start again. There is no jump.

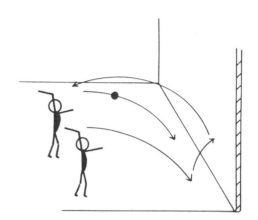

GAME 60
SPIKE ACTION, 2 PLAYERS, 1 BALL, WALL

Two players alternate spiking the ball to the floor and wall within a contained area. The object is to hit the ball to the floor in such a way as to force your opponent to miss the next contact. Start with a narrow court and then make it wider.

DRILL 61
SPIKE ACTION, 3 PLAYERS, ATTACKER BALL

Two players hold the attacker ball up at about head height. The spiker lifts both arms simulating the arm lift on the jump, touches the ball with the non-hitting hand while winding up the hitting hand and then whips back through to contact the ball. Emphasize the lift with both arms, a loose whipping action and follow through. Next raise the ball high enough to force the player to reach up to contact the ball (no jump). This should be held at the ideal contact height for the individual player.

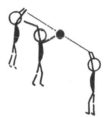

DRILL 62
SPIKE ACTION, 3 PLAYERS, ATTACKER BALL, 2 CHAIRS

Two players stand on chairs and hold the ball at the ideal hitting height for the spiker. (A) The spiker stands slightly away from the ball, squats and jumps using the proper arm action (no approach). (B) The spiker touches the ball with the non-hitting hand while winding up with the spiking hand and then whips to contact the ball. The spiker will jump slightly forward. Repeat 10 times and rotate.

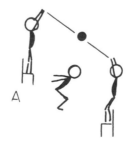
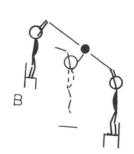

A   B

DRILL 63
SPIKE ACTION, 3 PLAYERS,
ATTACKER BALL, 2 CHAIRS

(A) Two players stand on chairs and hold the ball at the ideal hitting height for the spiker. (B) The spiker uses a one step approach, jumps and spikes the ball. Emphasize the arm swing and loose whipping action. Once the player has the approach and hitting technique mastered with a one step approach, an extra step or two can be added to the approach. The authors strongly recommend the use of a one step approach for beginning level players as the timing is much easier.

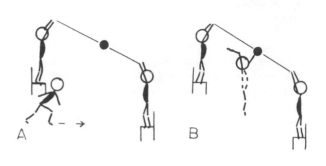

DRILL 64
SPIKE ACTION, 3 PLAYERS,
ATTACKER BALL, NET, 2 CHAIRS

Two players stand on chairs close to the net and hold the attacker ball up at the ideal hitting height for the individual spiker. The spiker uses a one or two step approach, jumps and spikes the ball. The spiker then moves backward to the attack line and repeats the action. Once the technique is done properly, speed up the recovery and approach.

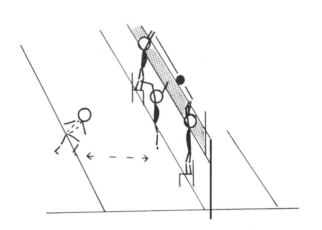

OBJECTIVE
To teach the spike approach
and jump

DRILL 65
SPIKE APPROACH, 1 PLAYER, NET,
3 STICKS

Place three sticks on the floor as indicated. The player steps over the first stick and hops over the second stick to land for the jump straddling the third stick as indicated. Note that this is for one style of approach and takeoff in which the spiker jumps facing toward the setter. Spread the sticks for a longer approach or add another stick for a longer approach. Take care to have hop step takeoff from the left foot as this has advantages in gaining an 'open stance' takeoff in relationship to the setter (for right-handed spiker).

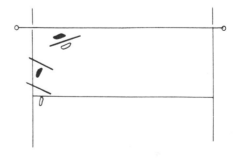

DRILL 66
SPIKE APPROACH, 1 PLAYER, NET, BENCH

Place a bench as indicted. The player now hops over the bench to land for the jump takeoff. At this stage one can land in an open stance to the setter (i.e., facing the setter) or in a semi-open stance more toward the net depending upon the point of view of the coach. Next have the student jump and takeoff with an emphasis on the footwork, crouch, arm swing and jump.

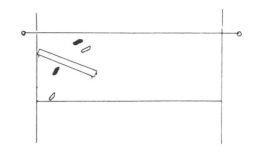

DRILL 67
SPIKE APPROACH, 1 PLAYER, TENNIS BALL, NET, BENCH

Place a bench as indicated. The player hops over the bench, jumps and throws the tennis ball over the net to the floor simulating the spiking action.

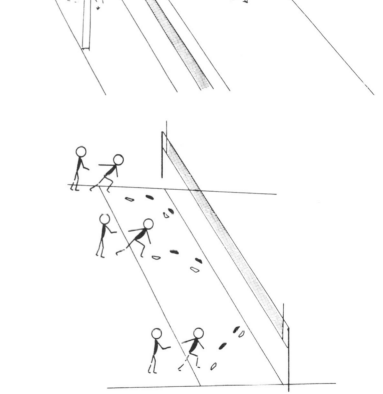

DRILL 68
SPIKE APPROACH, 2-20 PLAYERS, NET, FOOTPRINTS

Mark the desired placement of the feet for the approach and takeoff on the floor either as footprints, circles or x's. The players approach and jump at all three positions attempting to step on each footprint. Move the footprints for various angles of approach or for various lengths of stride. **Note:** Footprints are for right-handed spikers: right-left — right-left.

DRILL 69
SPIKE APPROACH, 1 PLAYER, TENNIS BALL, NET

The player starts the approach with a tennis ball in the non-hitting hand. On the jump, lift both arms above the head, switch the ball from the non-hitting hand to the hitting hand, and then throw the ball over the net simulating the spiking action. This is to emphasize the lift with both arms.

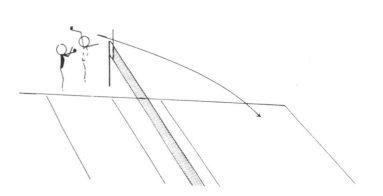

DRILL 70
SPIKE APPROACH, 2-20 PLAYERS,
3 BALLS, NET, 3 CHAIRS

Three players stand on the chairs close to the net and hold a ball high. The spikers approach and jump, using the desired footwork and arm swing, and grab the ball with both hands. Approach at all three positions.

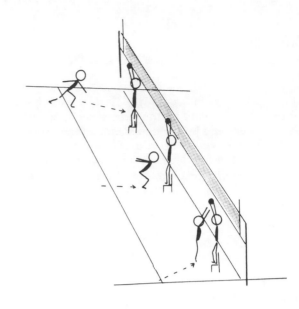

DRILL 71
SPIKE APPROACH, 2-20 PLAYERS,
3 BALLS, NET, 3 CHAIRS, 3 PYLONS

Three players stand on the chairs close to the net and hold a ball high. Pylons are placed beside the desired takeoff spot. The spiker must approach and jump from beside the pylon. The pylons may be positioned to the left or the right to force the player to jump and drift to the left or right so that the hitting shoulder is in line with the ball. The spiker grabs the ball with both hands.

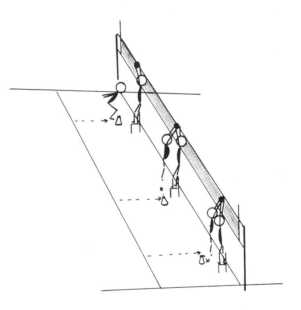

DRILL 72
SPIKE APPROACH, 2-20 PLAYERS,
10 BALLS, NET, 3 CHAIRS, 3 PYLONS

Three players stand on chairs close to the net and hold a ball high. Pylons are placed beside the desired takeoff spot. The spikers approach, jump and spike the ball from the hand of the player who is holding the ball. Players chase their own balls and return to a different spiking line.

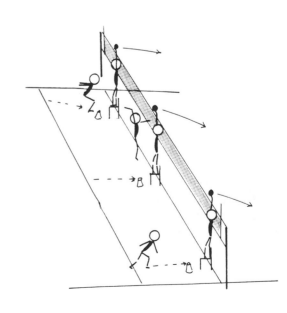

DRILL 73
SPIKE APPROACH, 3-20 PLAYERS,
10 BALLS, NET, 3 CHAIRS, 3 PYLONS

Three players stand on chairs close to the net and hold a ball high. Pylons are placed beside the desired takeoff spot. The spiker approaches, jumps and spikes the ball from the hand of the player who is holding the ball. The spiker than moves backward to beyond the attack line and repeats the approach and the attack while another player hands a second ball to the player on the chair.

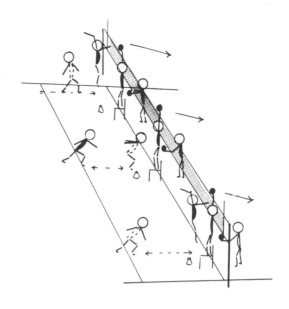

DRILL 74
SPIKE APPROACH, 2-20 PLAYERS,
3 BALLS, NET

Three players start at the net holding a ball high. As the spiker starts their approach, the person at the net takes a large step in any direction forcing the spiker to modify their approach so that their takeoff will be in line with the ball.

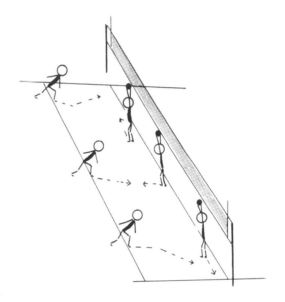

DRILL 75
SPIKE APPROACH, 2-20 PLAYERS,
3 BALLS, NET

Three players start at the net and toss balls straight up. The spiker approaches and jumps to catch the ball in both hands so that the ball is straight in front of and above the hitting shoulder. Once the player is jumping from the proper place, have the player toss the ball further out or at differing distances back from the net. The object is to have the player adjust their approach so that they are always in a good position to contact the ball.

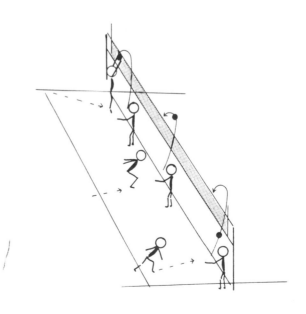

DRILL 76
SPIKE, 2-20 PLAYERS, BALLS, NET

Three players start at the net and toss balls straight up. The spikers approach and jump and spike the ball. Concentrate on jumping so that the ball is always above and in front of the hitting shoulder. Spikers chase their own balls and return to a different spiking line.

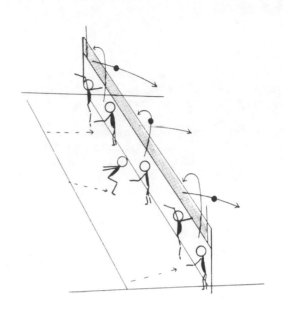

OBJECTIVE
To teach blocking hand action

DRILL 77
BLOCK, 2 PLAYERS, 1 BALL

One player stands about 2 metres in front of the other and lob spikes the ball towards the blocker's hands. The ball is blocked down.

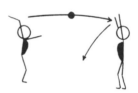

DRILL 78
BLOCK, 2 PLAYERS, 1 BALL, NET, BENCH

One player stands about 2 metres back from the net. The blocker stands on a bench on the other side of the net. The first player lob spikes or throws the ball directly towards the blocker's hands. The ball is blocked down. The same drill can be done without a bench by lowering the net so that the blocker can stand on the floor.

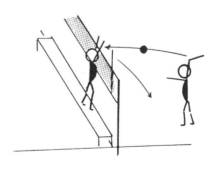

DRILL 79
BLOCK, 2 PLAYERS, 1 BALL, NET, BENCH, HOOP

Place a hoop on the floor on the attacker's side. The attacker stands about 2 metres back from the net. The blocker stands on a bench on the other side of the net. The ball is lob spiked towards the blocker's hands as they attempt to block the ball down to the hoop target.

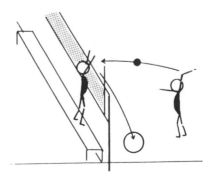

DRILL 80
BLOCK, 2 PLAYERS, 1 BALL, NET, BENCH

One player stands about 2 metres back from the net and lob spikes down the line or cross-court. The blocker stands on a bench on the other side of the net and must move to the left or right to intercept and block the ball. Start by having the attacker face the exact direction of the hit before hitting.

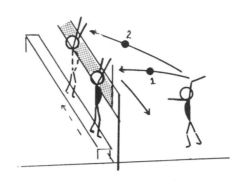

DRILL 81
BLOCK, 2 PLAYERS, 1 BALL, NET, CHAIR

One player stands on a chair and holds the ball above the head and close to the net. The blocker jumps, reaches over the net and pushes the ball out of the hands.

DRILL 82
BLOCK, 2 PLAYERS, 1 BALL, NET, CHAIR

One player stands on a chair and holds the ball above the head and close to the net. The blocker jumps, reaches over the net and tries to push the ball down to the floor. The other player holds the ball and pushes back.

DRILL 83
BLOCK, 2 PLAYERS, 1 BALL, NET, CHAIR, COACH

One player stands on a chair and holds the ball above the head and close to the net. The blocker jumps, reaches over the net and tries to push the ball down to the floor. As the player is blocking, the coach pushes the player slightly from behind while they are in the air. The blocker must learn to maintain balance.

DRILL 84
BLOCK, 10 PLAYERS, 1 BALL, NET,
2 BENCHES

Have 6 players stand on the benches, each holding a ball above and close to the net. The blocker must jump and push one ball, shift, jump and push the next ball, etc. This is to help with lateral movement and footwork. Repeat in both directions.

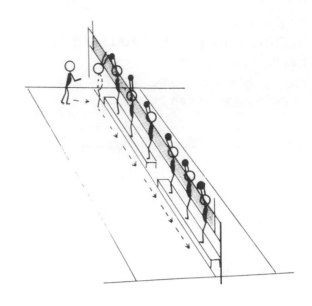

DRILL 85
BLOCK, 2 PLAYERS, 1 BALL, NET

One player jumps and holds the ball above the net. The blocker jumps, reaches over the net and attempts to push the ball down. The first player moves to the left or right and jumps again. The blocker must move with the other player and learn to follow the spiker.

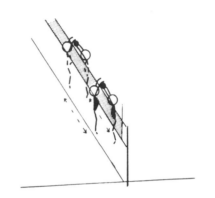

TO PRACTISE CARELESSLY
IS TO GO
BACKWARDS IN ABILITY.

OBJECTIVE
To teach the side slide and dig

DRILL 86
SIDE SLIDE TEACHING
PROGRESSION

Have the player lay on their side on the floor with the contact arm outstretched to feel how to contact the floor. Do on both sides.

By bending the top knee, planting the top foot and pushing, the player can slide along the floor.

The player sits on the floor and the coach tosses a ball to the side of the player. The player reaches to the side, digs the ball and rolls on the side. Do to both sides.

Place a ball on the floor 2 metres away. The player starts in a low crouch position with the left knee on the floor, weight lightly on the left hand, body leaning slightly to the right. Lean further and push with the right leg as you fall. Reach out with the right hand toward the ball. Do to both sides.

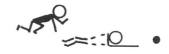

The player starts in a low crouch, hands on the floor. Step forward, reach, rotate and slide on the side.

One player tosses a ball low and to the side and in front of the digger. The digger starts in a low crouch position, steps out and reaches to dig the ball, rotates and slides on the side. Keep the toss low to force the player to stay low.

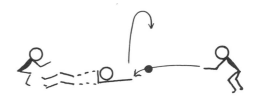

OBJECTIVE
To teach the roll and dig

DRILL 87
ROLL TEACHING PROGRESSION,
TUMBLING MAT, 1 BALL

The player does several backward rolls on the mat and then several backward shoulder rolls. Do the shoulder rolls to both sides. This is to teach the concept of rolling backward and also to warm up.

The player starts in a low ready defensive stance. Step out to the right side as far as possible, rotate on the right foot (toes), sit and roll onto the back. Do the same to the left. Be sure the body rotates over the toe. A long step or stride is also essential to get the body weight low.

Repeat the previous step and now rotate, sit and roll backward doing a backward shoulder roll. When stepping to the right, roll over the left shoulder. When stepping to the left, roll over the right shoulder.

Place a ball on the mat about one body length away. Step out to the right, scoop up the ball with the right hand, rotate and roll.

Once the player is comfortable with the roll, a partner can toss a ball to the side for the player to step out, dig, rotate and roll. The momentum from the swing of the hand as it contacts the ball will help with the rotation.

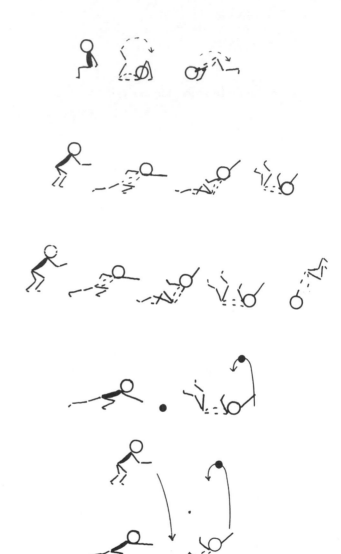

DRILL 88
DIG AND ROLL, 2 PLAYERS,
4 BALLS, MAT

Two players start about 4 metres apart. One player tosses balls alternately to the left and then the right forcing the player to step out, dig, roll, recover and then go to the other side. Continue. Start on a mat. Once the player has confidence, do the same drill on the floor. Toss low and force the player to extend to dig the ball. The tosser should lead the roller.

OBJECTIVE
To teach the forward dive and dig

DRILL 89
DIVE-CATCH-SLIDE:
TEACHING PROGRESSION

The player starts low on one knee in the "on your mark" posture with both hands touching the floor beside the knee. Rock forward, backward and then push off forward with the body close to the floor. Catch the body weight on the hands and pull the body ahead and slide on the abdomen.

The player starts in a low squat position. Take one or two steps keeping the body low and dive out, catch and slide. The key points are to keep low and to have forward momentum.

The player does the same as in the previous step and now immediately recovers to the feet and repeats the dive again several times in a row across the gym floor. Stay low and move quickly.

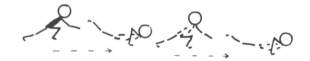

The player does the same as in the previous step except that they now step out in different directions each time.

Once the player feels confident and comfortable in sliding, have a partner toss a ball ahead for the player to dig before the catch and slide. Be sure to keep the toss low and force the player to extend while diving.

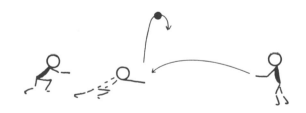

DRILL 90
DIVE-CATCH-SLIDE,
2 PLAYERS, 3 BALLS

One player tosses a ball for a player to dive, dig and slide. The tosser immediately tosses a second ball for the player to dive and dig, and then repeat with a third ball. The tosser will have to move with the diver to better place the toss. Be sure to keep the toss low and to toss well in front of the diver.

NOTES

PART III

BASIC SKILL

DEVELOPMENT DRILLS

OBJECTIVE
To develop serving accuracy

DRILL 91
SERVE, 4 PLAYERS, 2 BALLS, NET

Two players alternate serving to two players who alternate passing. The passers are on each side of the court to force the server to serve line and then cross-court. As soon as the player passes, they catch the ball and roll it to the server, and then change places with the other passer. After 15 serves, rotate from passers to servers.

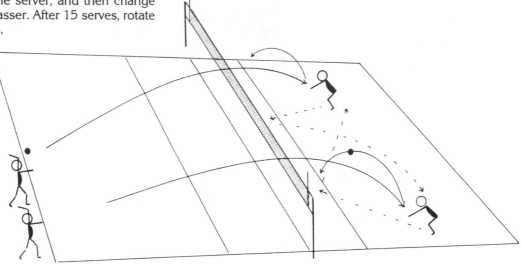

DRILL 92
SERVE, 4 PLAYERS, 2 BALLS, NET

Two players alternate serving and two players alternate receiving. The passers are on each side of the court to force the server to serve line and then cross-court. While one player passes, the other player acts as the setter target, catches the ball, rolls it back to the setter, and then moves to receive the serve. Have the servers change from line to cross-court after 15 serves and then rotate from servers to passers after another 15 serves.

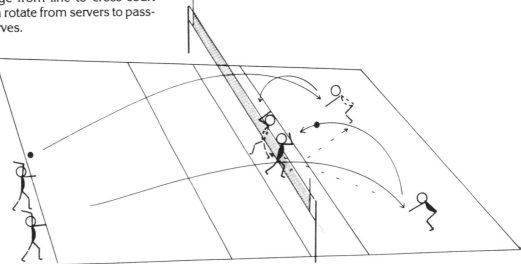

DRILL 93
SERVE, PASS, SET, 4 PLAYERS,
2 BALLS, NET

Two players alternate serving and two players alternate receiving. While one player passes, the other moves to set and the passer then moves to either tip, lob spike or spike the ball back to the servers. After setting, you pass. After tipping, you set. Move the receivers to various places on the court. Rotate from servers to passers.

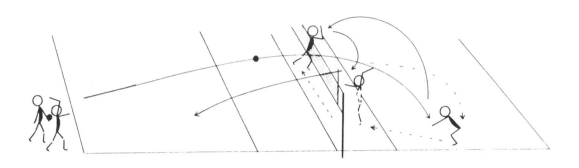

DRILL 94
SERVE, PASS, SET, SPIKE,
4 PLAYERS, 2 BALLS, NET

Two players alternate serving and two players alternate receiving. While one player passes, the other moves to set and the passer then moves to spike or tip the ball back at the server. After serving, the player moves into court to dig the spike or tip. Catch the ball and move back to serve again. Rotate from servers to passers.

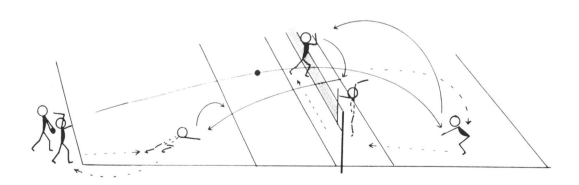

GAME 95
SERVE, 6-12 PLAYERS, 10 BALLS,
NET, 2 CHAIRS, 2 BENCHES

Place one bench on each side of the net and about 1 metre away from the side line. Place one chair on each side of the net and close to the back corner of the court as indicated.

Form teams of 3 to 6 players per team and alternate serving to the target. Score +5 if the serve hits the chair and +3 if the serve lands between the bench and the side line. The first team to hit 45 is the winner.

Another way to keep score is to award -2 or -1 (depending upon the skill level of the players) for each miss and the winner is the first to +15.

GAME 96
SERVE, 6-12 PLAYERS,
20 BALLS, 6 CHAIRS

Place 3 chairs on each side of the net close to the back line as indicated. Form teams of 3 to 6 players per team or serve as individuals. In a team situation serve to hit each chair in a sequence. Once a chair is hit, turn it over. The first team to 'knock down' all of the targets is the winner.

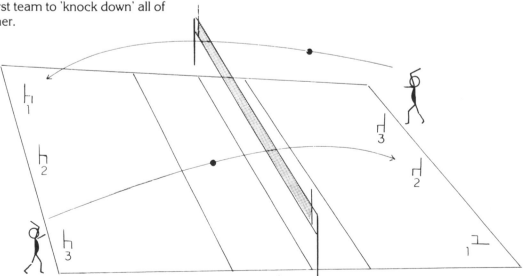

GAME 97
SERVE, 6-12 PLAYERS,
20 BALLS, TAPE OR ROPE

Mark a target on the court as indicated. The back corners are the toughest to hit and should have the highest value. The middle is the easiest to hit and should have the lowest value. Set a goal of 45 or have each player serve 15 and keep a running score with the player with the highest total declared the winner. Set up teams with partners.

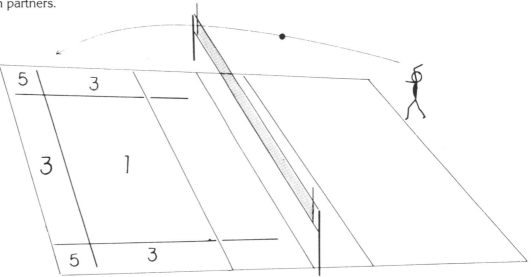

DRILL 98
SERVE, 2-12 PLAYERS,
20 BALLS, NET, 2 CHAIRS

Two players serve from opposite serving areas. The chairs are set up at various places on the court according to the scouting report you have on your next opponents. The player serves around the chair to avoid hitting the target thus simulating forcing the receiver to move to pass the serve. A player serves 15 balls in succession and then change. The extra players chase balls and feed them to the servers. The coach may put the opponent's shirt numbers on the chairs or whistle before each serve to create game-like situations.

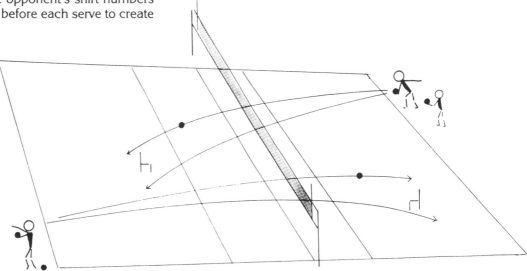

DRILL 99
SERVE, PASS, 6 PLAYERS,
20 BALLS, NET

This is the same as the previous drill except that a player is used to pass serve and a setter receives the pass and sets. Force the passer to move to the limits of their area. The passer will move to different areas. The extra players chase balls and feed them to the server.

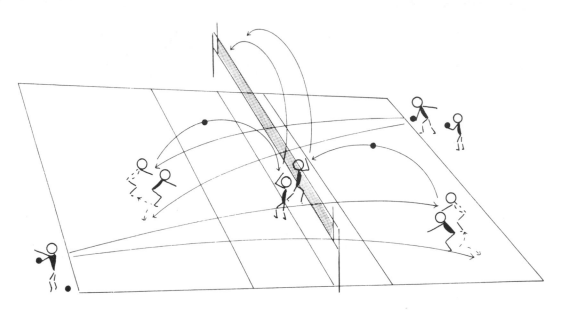

LACK OF CONCENTRATION
IS
MENTAL LOAFING.

OBJECTIVE
To teach the player to absorb
the force of a spiked ball

DRILL 100
FOREARM DIG, 2 PLAYERS, 1 BALL

One player assumes a low posture for the forearm pass with the arms out in front, straight and well away from the body. The other player holds a ball against the forearms and presses on the ball. The player relaxes the shoulders to absorb the force without bending the arms. Note that the arms are pushed back by the ball, not pulled back by the player.

DRILL 101
FOREARM DIG, 2 PLAYERS,
1 BALL, BENCH

One player stands about 3 metres in front of the other player who is seated on a bench, knees apart, body leaning forward and arms in front of the body. The standing player throws or hits a ball directly at the outstretched forearms of the seated player who attempts to absorb the entire force of the ball at the shoulders and not let the ball bounce more than one metre away from the arms.

DRILL 102
FOREARM DIG, 2 PLAYERS, 1 BALL

One player stands about 3 metres in front of the other and throws or hits the ball directly at the outstretched forearms of the other player (who is crouched low). The player attempts to absorb the entire force of the ball at the shoulders and not let the ball bounce more than one metre away from the arms.

OBJECTIVE
To teach a player to get low on defense

DRILL 103
DIG, 2 PLAYERS, 1 BALL

The digger kneels on one knee, weight forward with both hands out in front of the body and very close to the floor. One player hits balls at half speed to a place in front of the digger. The digger plays the ball with one or both hands, and will normally continue to fall forward, catching the body weight on one or both hands after digging the ball.

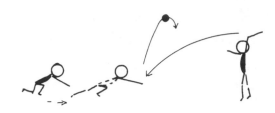

DRILL 104
DIG, 2 PLAYERS, 1 BALL

Two players start 4 metres apart. One player hits to a place in front or to the side of the digger. The digger starts in a 3 point football stance and dives out to dig the ball.

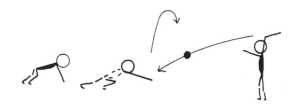

DRILL 105
DIG, 2 PLAYERS, 1 BALL

Two players start 4 metres apart. One player hits to a place in front or to the side of the digger. (A) As the hitter tosses the ball up, the digger hops to a low squat and touches the floor with one or both hands before (B) reacting to dig the ball.

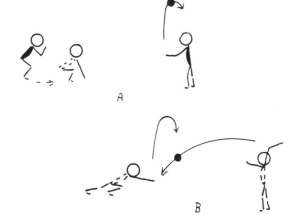

DRILL 106
DIG, 4 PLAYERS, 2 BALLS, NET, PLATFORM

One player stands on the platform and spikes at either one of two players who alternate digging. The ball should be hit low for the player to dig towards a fourth player who catches the ball and feeds it to the hitter.

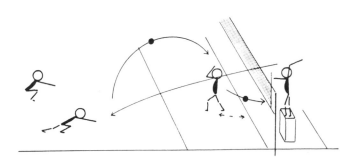

DRILL 107
DIG, SET, 5 PLAYERS, 5 BALLS, NET, PLATFORM

One player stands on the platform and spikes. The other players, in pairs, play defense. The ball is hit low to one player to dig and the partner runs under the pass and sets. The digger then moves to catch the set and feed it to the hitter. The next two partners do the same and repeat. Be sure to spike low, aiming at the ankles or knees of the defensive player.

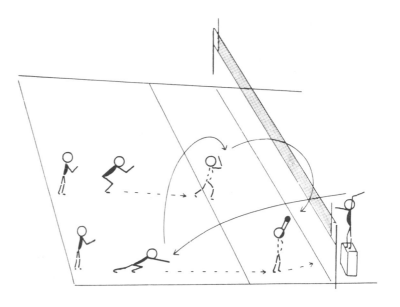

OBJECTIVE
To learn to dig a tipped ball toward the setter

DRILL 108
DIG, 3 PLAYERS, 2 BALLS, NET

One player stands in front of the net and tips a ball to midcourt. The defensive player stands close to the back line, dives, slides or rolls while digging the ball toward a third target player standing at the setting place. Recover and repeat rapidly. Repeat from all three back-court positions.

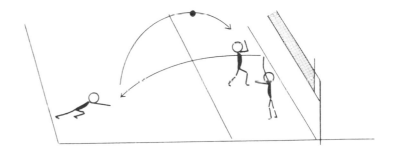

DRILL 109
DIG, 3 PLAYERS, 2 BALLS, NET, CHAIR

One player stands on a chair on the other side of the net and tips for a defensive player to dig to a third player standing at the setting place. The third player then feeds the ball to the tipper.

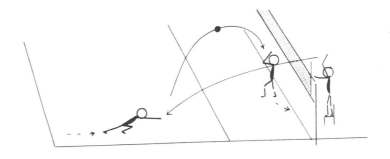

DRILL 110
DIG, 7-9 PLAYERS, 10 BALLS, NET

Three attackers alternate tossing a ball up and tipping over the net. Three defensive players start in the three back court positions and dig all balls tipped to their area. The dig is passed to a player in the setting place who catches the ball and throws it to the respective tipper. Repeat as rapidly as possible. The extra players chase balls and feed the tippers.

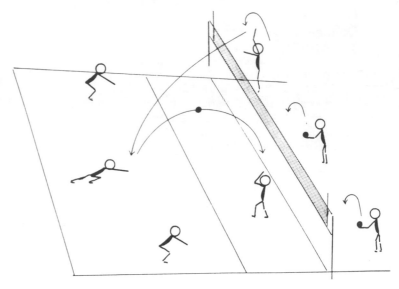

DRILL 111
DIG, 6-10 PLAYERS, 10 BALLS, NET, PLATFORM

One player stands on a platform and tips over the net to various places on the court. One player stands as a target in the setting place, catches balls and feeds them to the feeder. One player feeds balls to the tipper. The other players take turns digging the tipped ball to the target. Repeat the drill by starting in all three back-court positions. Other players chase balls.

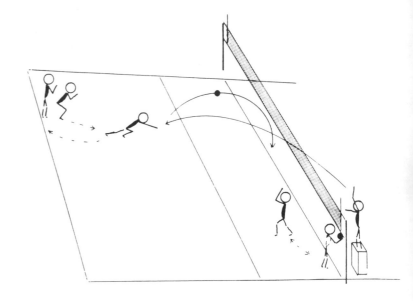

OBJECTIVE
To improve forearm passing skills

DRILL 112
FOREARM PASS, OVERHAND PASS, 2 PLAYERS, 1 BALL

Players start about 3 metres apart. One player overhand passes low to the second player who passes high back to the first player using a forearm pass. Start by passing accurately to the second passer and then force the player to move from side to side before making the forearm pass.

DRILL 113
FOREARM PASS, OVERHAND PASS,
2 PLAYERS, 1 BALL

Players start about 5 metres apart. One player is stationary and overhand passes low to the second player forcing the player to move forward to make the pass. The passer then moves back and then forward again before each pass. Try to bump the ball accurately to the upstretched hands of the setter.

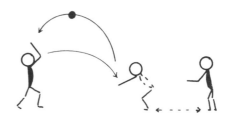

DRILL 114
FOREARM PASS, 2 PLAYERS, 1 BALL

One player is stationary and tosses the ball over the other player's head, forcing that player to move backward to make the pass. In this drill, it is easier to move a longer distance and pass the ball from the side of the body than to move back and pass the ball from in front of the body. The passer must move back quickly, plant the front foot, pivot and turn the body to the side, dip the shoulder and pass. Practice passing from both sides of the body. Start with a high toss and then gradually lower the toss to make the movement more difficult.

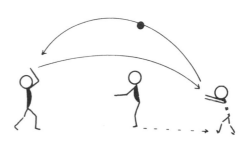

DRILL 115
FOREARM PASS, 2 PLAYERS, 1 BALL,
NET

One player stands behind the attack line and the other starts on the other side of the net about 1 metre back from the net. The player sets the ball low forcing the other player to move forward, duck under the net and pass back to the upstretched hands of the setter. It may be necessary to lower the net on this drill to force players to get low.

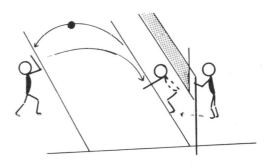

DRILL 116
FOREARM PASS, 2 PLAYERS, 1 BALL

Two players start about 3 metres apart. One player tips the ball. The other moves under the ball and passes it accurately up to the first player to tip again.

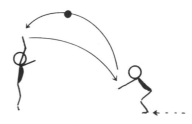

DRILL 117
FOREARM PASS, 3 PLAYERS, 1 BALL

Three players start about 3 metres apart in a triangle. The first player sets, the second player tips and the third player passes (forearm pass) back to the first player. Continue. Attempt to do as many successful sequences in a row as possible.

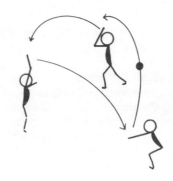

DRILL 118
FOREARM PASS, 3 PLAYERS, 1 BALL, NET

The setter starts close to the net and sets the ball high over the net for the second player to tip to the third player who passes accurately back to the setter. Start by tipping accurately to the passer and then make the passer move by tipping long or short or to the side.

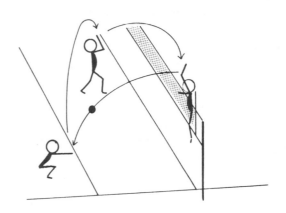

GAME 119
FOREARM PASS, TIP AND SET,
3 PLAYERS, 1 BALL, NET

The passer and the setter are on one side of the net and the tipper is on the other side of the net. The passer must pass the ball up to the setter who sets high over the net for the tipper to tip. The setter is a neutral player. The objective is for the tipper to force the passer to make a mistake. The passer scores one point each time they are able to pass the ball to the setter. The tipper scores one point each time the passer is unable to make a pass to the setter. Start by confining the area open to the tip to of the court, then of the court. Play to 15 points and then rotate positions.

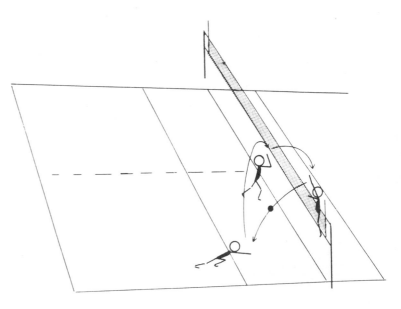

DRILL 120
FOREARM DIG, 2 PLAYERS, 1 BALL

The defensive player moves forward or to the side with a short step and hop into a 'split step' or low stance with the feet shoulder width apart, and the body facing more to the middle of the court. The outside foot should be ahead, knees bent and body posture low. Do this several times until the player is in a good low posture with the arms in front ready to dig. Next the other player will hit the ball accurately and at half speed directly at the forearms of the defensive player. The defensive player absorbs the force of the ball with loose shoulders, hips and knees, but keeps the arms straight and facing slightly in toward the middle of the court.

DRILL 121
FOREARM DIG, 2 PLAYERS, 1 BALL

The attacker spikes the ball at half speed slightly in front of or to the side of the defensive player. The defensive player hops into the low stance and passes the ball back to the spiker. Gradually increase the speed of the spike.

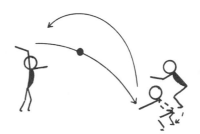

DRILL 122
FOREARM DIG, 2 PLAYERS, 1 BALL

The attacker spikes the ball at half speed slightly to the left (or right) of the defensive players and then moves in the opposite direction one or two steps to become a target for the dig. The defensive player must plant their feet so that the outside foot is ahead and the body is turned to face the target before digging the ball. Merely allow the ball to rebound in the direction of the target. Gradually increase the speed of the spike.

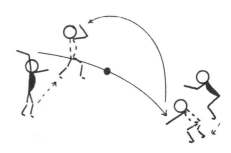

DRILL 123
FOREARM DIG, 3 PLAYERS, 1 BALL, NET

One player tosses the ball up for an attacker to spike directly at a defensive player on the other side of the net. The tosser crosses under the net after the toss and becomes the target for the return dig. Rotate after 10 hits. Ensure that the defensive player is positioned properly and absorbing the force of the spike with the shoulders, hips and knees, and also turned in to face the target.

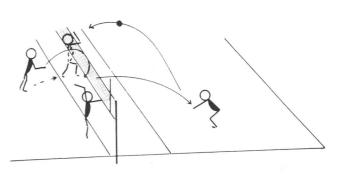

DRILL 124
FOREARM DIG, 3 PLAYERS, COACH,
10 BALLS, NET, PLATFORM

The coach stands on the platform and spikes balls at the defensive player who must move in, plant, crouch and dig the ball toward a second player who acts as a target. A third player feeds balls to the coach. Allow the defensive player to recover and move in again for each spike. Do this drill with both line and cross-court spikes from both sides of the court. Rotate after 10 hits. Start slow and with half-speed hits and gradually pick up the speed and also the force of the spike.

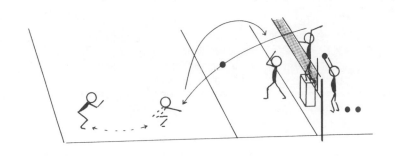

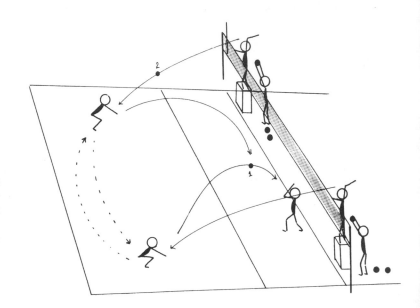

DRILL 125
FOREARM DIG, 7 PLAYERS,
10 BALLS, NET, 2 PLATFORMS

Two players stand on the platforms, one on each side of the court, and spike line alternately at the two defensive players. The defensive players attempt to dig the ball up to the target player at the net. After digging on one side of the court, they move to dig on the other side of the court. Ensure that the feet are positioned correctly to turn the ball back into the middle of the court and to face the target.

OBJECTIVE
To develop proper body position
and feet alignment when passing

DRILL 126
PASS, 2 PLAYERS, 1 BALL

Two players start 4 metres apart. One player tosses the ball up to the left or right of the passer. The passer must move under the ball and plant so that the feet and body are aligned directly to the tosser, and pass back to the tosser. The tosser could remain stationary and pass rather than toss.

DRILL 127
PASS, 2 PLAYERS, 1 BALL, NET

The tosser starts close to the net in the setting place. The passer starts at the net. The ball is tossed up behind the attack line and the passer must move back from the net and plant so that the feet and body are aligned directly to the tosser, and pass back to the tosser. Start with a high toss to give the passer enough time to plant, and then lower the height of the toss to make it more difficult.

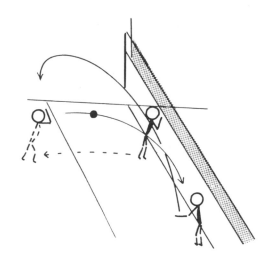

DRILL 128
PASS, 2 PLAYERS, 1 BALL

Two players start one metre apart facing each other. The tosser throws the ball up forcing the passer to move back, plant, and then pass back to the tosser. Gradually make it more difficult by tossing the ball further or lower.

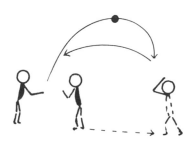

DRILL 129
PASS, 2 PLAYERS, 1 BALL

The players start side by side. The tosser throws a ball up high and the passer must run under the ball, turn and align the feet and body up with the tosser and pass back to the tosser.

DRILL 130
PASS, 2 PLAYERS, 1 BALL

One player tosses a ball up high and runs to a new place and shouts "here". The passer moves under the ball, turns to face the tosser and passes to the tosser. Gradually toss the ball further to make the pass more difficult.

OBJECTIVE
To improve overhand passing skills

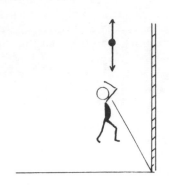

DRILL 131
OVERHAND PASS, 1 PLAYER, 1 BALL, WALL

The player stands close to the wall and passes the ball straight up without the ball touching the wall. Do 10 or 20 passes in succession.

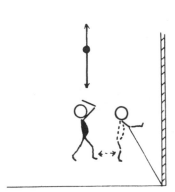

DRILL 132
OVERHAND PASS, 1 PLAYER, 1 BALL, WALL

The player stands about 2 metres away from the wall and passes the ball high straight up, moves to touch the wall and back to make the next pass. Do 10 or 20 passes in succession.

DRILL 133
OVERHAND PASS, 1 PLAYER, 1 BALL, WALL

The player starts about 1 metre away from the wall and passes the ball to the wall continuously while moving to one side down the length of the wall. Return in the opposite direction.

DRILL 134
OVERHAND PASS, 1 PLAYER, 1 BALL, WALL

The player starts 5 metres away from the wall, bounces the ball on the floor, moves under the ball and passes it to a target on the wall.

GAME 135
OVERHAND PASS, 1 PLAYER, 1 BALL, LINES ON WALL

Mark lines on the wall at heights of 3 metres, 4 metres and 5 metres. The player attempts to pass the ball to the wall above the top line. Keep score on 15 consecutive passes — 3 points for 5 metres, 2 points for 4 metres and 1 point for 3 metres.

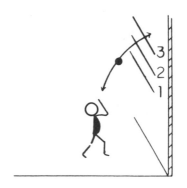

GAME 136
OVERHAND PASS, 1 PLAYER, 1 BALL, TARGET ON WALL

Mark a circle or square on the wall about 4 metres above the floor — the higher the skill level, the smaller the circle. The player attempts to pass to the circle 15 times in a row without missing. Have players compete to see who scores highest out of 15 passes.

DRILL 137
OVERHAND PASS, 1 PLAYER, 1 BALL, WALL

The player starts about 2 metres away from the wall and passes the ball high to the wall and jumps to make the next 'jump set'. Attempt to do 15 or 30 passes in succession. Catch the ball and start again when you lose control.

DRILL 138
OVERHAND PASS, 1 PLAYER, 1 BALL

The player passes the ball 3 metres above their head and about 1 metre in front, steps forward under the ball and repeats the action. Continue. Then gradually pass the ball further in front thereby increasing the difficulty. Ask the player to move fast under the ball and be ready early to make the pass.

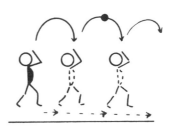

DRILL 139
OVERHAND PASS, 20 PLAYERS, 20 BALLS

The players pass the ball above their heads continuously in time with the cadence shouted or whistled by the coach/teacher. A long, slow cadence results in high passes, while a short quick cadence results in low passes. This same drill can be done using a forearm pass or alternating between a forearm pass and an overhand pass.

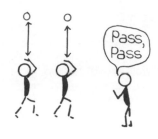

DRILL 140
OVERHAND PASS, 1 PLAYER, 1 BALL

The player passes the ball high above their head, does a half turn, or a full turn and passes again. Reverse turning directions each time.

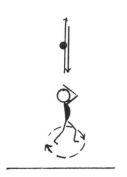

DRILL 141
OVERHAND PASS, 1 PLAYER, 1 BALL

The player passes the ball above their head continuously and gradually kneels and then sits on the floor and then lays on the floor on their back. Slowly reverse the process while continuously passing the ball.

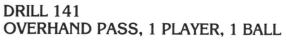

DRILL 142
OVERHAND PASS, 20 PLAYERS, 20 BALLS

The players pass the ball above their heads continuously and follow the commands of the coach/teacher: "walk forward, walk backward, turn 90 degrees, turn 180 degrees, kneel, sit, lie on your back, stand up, walk, jump, run, etc."

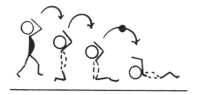

DRILL 143
OVERHAND PASS, 1 PLAYER,
1 BALL, LINE ON FLOOR

The player starts on one side of a line on the floor and passes the ball back and forth high across the line. The player steps over the line, turns and passes the ball back. Start with high passes to allow time and then gradually make it more difficult with lower passes.

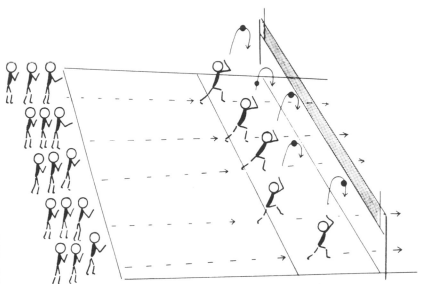

GAME 144
OVERHAND PASS, 20 PLAYERS,
5 BALLS

Relay race. Four players per team. Start at one side or end of the court. The players must pass the ball continuously and run across the court and back, and pass to the next player on their team. Run the length of the court and force the player to pass over the net on the way down and under the net on the way back (low squat) or do a 360 degree turn at each line, or sit at each line, all the while passing the ball to themselves. This game can also be done with the forearm pass or a combination of the two passing styles.

DRILL 145
OVERHAND PASS, 1 PLAYER, 1 BALL,
NET

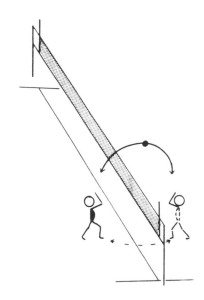

The player passes the ball high, back and forth over the net. The player crosses under the net, turns and passes the ball back. Start with high passes to allow more time and then gradually make it more difficult with lower passes.

DRILL 146
OVERHAND PASS, 1 PLAYER, 1 BALL, NET

The player passes the ball high, back and forth over the net. The player passes the ball forward from one side of the net, crosses forward under the net and passes the ball back using a back set then moves backward under the net and continues. Try to make 15 passes or 30 passes without a mistake.

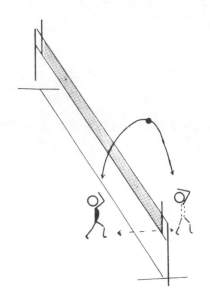

DRILL 147
OVERHAND PASS, 1 PLAYER, 1 BALL, NET

The player starts beside and close to the net and passes the ball above the head and slightly forward while moving forward along the net. Do the same thing while moving backward along the net. Keep close to the net.

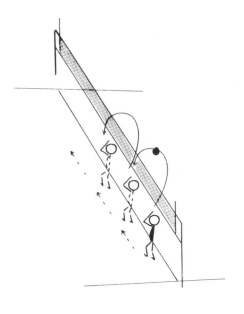

DRILL 148
OVERHAND PASS, 1 PLAYER, 1 BALL, NET

The player starts at one end of and close to the net. The ball is passed back and forth over the net as the player moves forward in a zig-zag fashion while crossing under the net with each pass. Turn and return as you reach the end of the net.

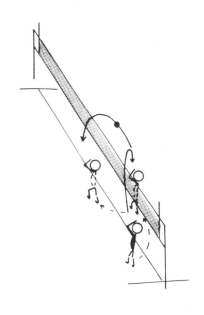

DRILL 149
OVERHAND PASS, 2 PLAYERS, 1 BALL

Two players start about 2 metres apart and pass low back and forth without lowering the hands away from the forehead.

DRILL 150
OVERHAND PASS, 2 PLAYERS, 1 BALL

Two players start about 2 metres apart and pass the ball back and forth without lowering the hands away from the forehead. Pass slightly to the side in one direction each time and then to the side in the other direction each time so that the players move down the gym floor.

DRILL 151
OVERHAND PASS, 2 PLAYERS, 1 BALL

Two players start about 2 metres apart and pass the ball back and forth. One player remains stationary and passes the ball so that the other player must move back to pass and then forward to pass.

DRILL 152
OVERHAND PASS, 2 PLAYERS, 1 BALL

Two players start about 2 metres apart and pass the ball back and forth. One player moves backward while the other player moves forward along the length of the gym.

DRILL 153
OVERHAND PASS, 2 PLAYERS, 1 BALL

Two players start about 2 metres apart and pass the ball back and forth. One player remains stationary while the other circles around the stationary player. The pass to the stationary player must be accurate. Gradually force the moving player to move further or to make longer passes.

DRILL 154
OVERHAND PASS, 2 PLAYERS, 1 BALL

Two players start about 3 metres apart. One player tosses the ball up and the other player moves under the ball to pass. Meanwhile the tosser moves and shouts and the passer must turn and pass accurately to the tosser. Catch and toss again. Later have the tosser and the passer both pass and move and shout.

DRILL 155
OVERHAND PASS, 2 PLAYERS, 1 BALL

Two players start about 3 metres apart and about 2 metres away from a wall or the net. They pass the ball back and forth and after each pass they must move and touch the wall or net and return to make the next pass. Gradually make the distance greater.

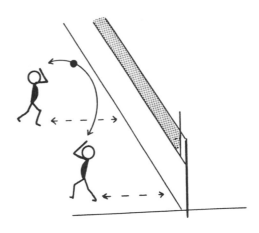

DRILL 156
OVERHAND PASS, 1 PLAYER, 1 BALL, BASKETBALL BASKET

The player tosses the ball up and passes to the basket from somewhere inside the key. A set from the free throw line is about the same distance as a normal front set. Move around and set from different places.

DRILL 157
OVERHAND PASS, 1 PLAYER, 1 BALL, BASKETBALL BASKET

The player bounces the ball on the floor, moves under the ball and passes to the basket. Bounce the ball low and squat to make the set, or bounce the ball high and jump to make the set.

DRILL 158
OVERHAND PASS, 2 PLAYERS, 1 BALL, BASKETBALL BASKET

One player tosses the ball up and the other player must move under the ball and set to the basket. Start with an easy distance and then move further away from the basket.

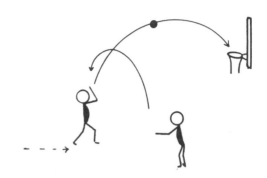

DRILL 159
OVERHAND PASS, 2 PLAYERS, 1 BALL, BASKETBALL BASKET

One player tosses the ball up above the free throw line. The passer starts outside of the key, moves in under the ball, and passes to the basket. Gradually increase the distance the passer must move, or have the passer sit on the floor to start.

DRILL 160
OVERHAND PASS, 2 PLAYERS, 1 BALL, BASKETBALL BASKET

One player tosses the ball up above the free throw line. The passer starts under the basket, moves out under the ball and sets backward to the basket. Toss the ball high to begin with and gradually lower to make it more difficult for the setter.

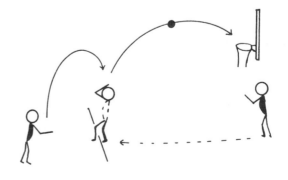

GAME 161
OVERHAND PASS, 2-4 PLAYERS,
2-4 BALLS, BASKETBALL BASKET

Golf. Identify 9 places (holes) around the key from which to pass to the basket. Each player takes turns tossing the ball up and passing to the basket from each place or hole. Keep a running total score of the number of attempts from each hole.

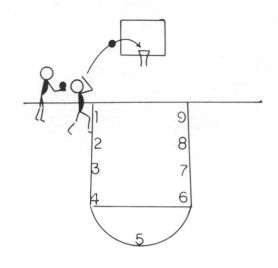

GAME 162
OVERHAND PASS, 2-4 PLAYERS,
2-4 BALLS, BASKETBALL BASKET

H.O.R.S.E. The first player tosses the ball up from any place they chose and sets to the basket. If the set is made, the next player must duplicate that style of pass from that place. If they make the set, the next player in turn must also duplicate the set. If they miss the set, they receive a penalty point (in this case the letters of the word 'horse') and the next player now has a choice of sets. Once a player has received 5 penalty points, (spelled out "horse') they are eliminated from the game.

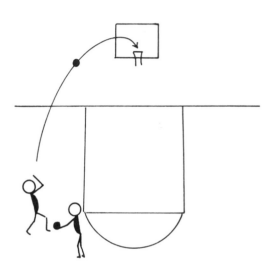

GAME 163
SERVE, PASS, 12 PLAYERS,
12 BALLS, 2 BASKETBALL BASKETS

Two teams of six with one team at each basket. The players, in turn, stand at the free throw line, serve against the backboard, and move in to pass the rebound into the basket. Score 2 points per basket and either play to 6 points or have a time limit.

DRILL 164
OVERHAND PASS, 3 PLAYERS, 1 BALL

Three players stand in a line about 4 metres apart. The middle player always sets backward. The outside players always set forward. An outside player starts by passing to the middle player who sets backward to the other outside player. The outside player then passes back to the middle player who has turned and who then passes backward to the first player. Change when the middle player becomes dizzy. Do this drill beside the net to encourage control.

DRILL 165
OVERHAND PASS, 3 PLAYERS, 1 BALL

Three players stand in a line about 4 metres apart. One outside player passes short to the middle player. The middle player passes backward to the other outside player. That player then passes long back to the first outside player. Gradually increase the distance between the players. Do this drill beside a net to encourage control.

DRILL 166
OVERHAND PASS, 3 PLAYERS, 1 BALL

Three players start in a line about 4 metres apart. One outside player starts by passing forward to the middle player, and then moves to change places with the middle player. The middle player, meanwhile, sets backward to the other outside player and then moves to change places with the first passer. The second outside player passes back to the middle player after the middle player has set backward to the outside. Continue.

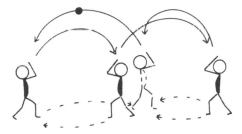

DRILL 167
OVERHAND PASS, 3 PLAYERS, 1 BALL, NET

Three players stand in a line close to the net. One outside player passes short to the middle player. The middle player passes backward to the other outside player. That player then passes long back to the first outside player. After passing, each player must move to the side to the attack line and then back in to make the next pass.

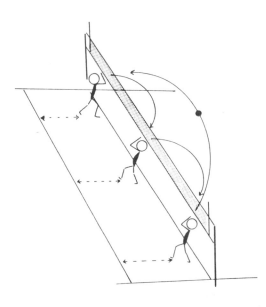

DRILL 168
OVERHAND PASS, 3 PLAYERS,
1 BALL, NET

Three players stand in a line close to the net. All passes are jump sets. One outside player passes short to the middle player who sets backward to the other outside player. That outside player then passes long back to the first player. Start about 3 metres apart and then gradually spread further apart to require longer passes.

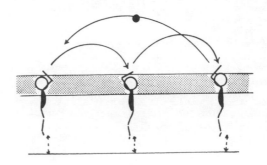

DRILL 169
OVERHAND PASS, 3 PLAYERS,
1 BALL, NET

The middle player starts on the attack line at midcourt. The outside players start close to the net, one at each side of the court. One outside player starts by setting the ball high to the middle. The middle player must move under the ball, turn and face the second outside player, and set to that player. The middle player then moves out to the attack line, moves back to the net and sets the return pass to the first player. Start by having the middle player only move a short distance and then have them eventually move out beyond the attack line. The purpose of this drill is to have the setter learn to turn under a ball and face the target before setting.

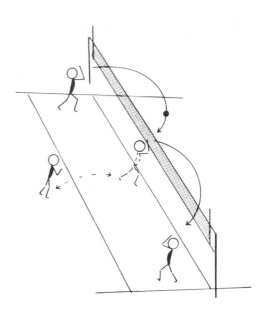

OBJECTIVE
To improve concentration
while passing

DRILL 170
PASS, 2 PLAYERS, 2 BALLS

The players pass the two balls back and forth simultaneously. The two balls will pass side by side and the players will move slightly left and right to pass. A variation is to have one partner pass slightly higher than the other, and reverse every 5 passes.

DRILL 171
PASS, 4 PLAYERS, 2 BALLS

Players start in a square and start passing back and forth in pairs. Start with high passes and pass the two balls simultaneously. Then after each pass exchange places with the player beside and keep passing simultaneously.

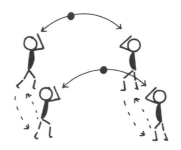

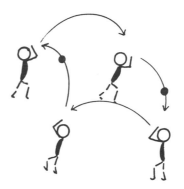

DRILL 172
PASS, 4 PLAYERS, 2 BALLS

Players start in a square about 4 metres apart. Two players in opposite corners start passing the two balls around the square in the same direction. Move closer together or lower the height of the pass to make the drill more difficult. Move further apart and try 3 balls or 4 balls.

DRILL 173
PASS, 8 PLAYERS, 2 BALLS, NET

Four players on each side of the net to start: one in position #4, one in position #2, and two in position #6 with the front players in position #6 with balls. The balls are passed from position #6, to position #2, to position #4, and over the net to position #6. As soon as the player passes, they move to take the position of the player to whom they passed. Keep the two balls going simultaneously by adjusting the height of the pass from time to time when necessary to speed it up or slow it down.

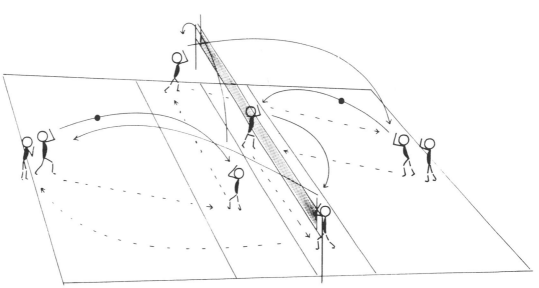

DRILL 174
PASS, TIP, 8 PLAYERS, 2 BALLS,
NET

Same as previous drill except that the player in position #4 now tips the ball over the net deep to position #6.

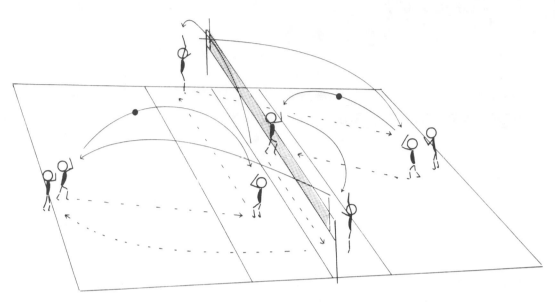

DRILL 175
PASS, TIP, BLOCK, 8 PLAYERS,
2 BALLS, NET

Same as previous drill except that the player in position #2 also blocks after setting and then runs to tip. It is important to try to keep the two balls being passed or tipped simultaneously.

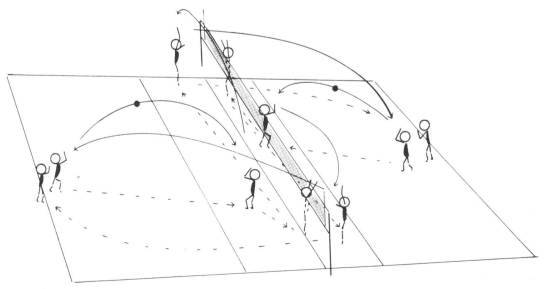

OBJECTIVE

To learn to recover and make an accurate overhand pass

DRILL 176
OVERHAND PASS, 1 PLAYER, 1 BALL, WALL

The player starts about 2 metres away from the wall and passes the ball high to the wall, turns or does a push up, and then passes the ball again.

DRILL 177
OVERHAND PASS, 2 PLAYERS, 1 BALL

Two players stand about 3 metres apart and pass the ball back and forth. After each pass the player must touch the floor with the hands or kneel and then make the next pass.

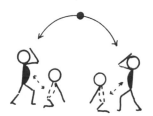

DRILL 178
OVERHAND PASS, 2 PLAYERS, 1 BALL

Two players start about 3 metres apart and pass the ball back and forth. After each pass they must turn 360 degrees and pass again, or turn 180 degrees and turn back and pass again.

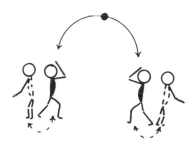

DRILL 179
OVERHAND PASS, 2 PLAYERS, 1 BALL

Two players start about 3 metres apart and pass the ball back and forth. After each pass the players must sit or do a push up, recover and make the next pass. High passes will be necessary at first. Gradually lower the height of the pass.

OBJECTIVE
To improve passing and setting skills

DRILL 180
FOREARM PASS, 4 PLAYERS,
2 BALLS, NET

One player serves from midcourt. Two players alternate passing to a setter who catches the ball and rolls it back to the server. Use two balls and serve as rapidly as possible. Gradually move the server back.

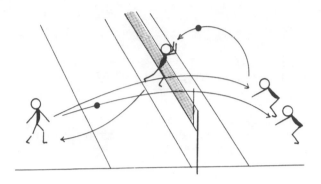

DRILL 181
FOREARM PASS, SET, 4 PLAYERS,
2 BALLS, NET

One player serves from mid-court. Two players alternate passing to a setter who sets for the passer to overhand pass the ball over the net to the server. Use two balls and serve rapidly. Gradually move the server back.

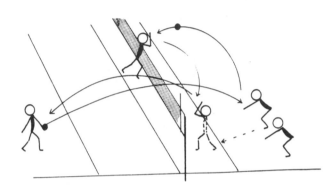

DRILL 182
FOREARM PASS, SET, LOB SPIKE,
4 PLAYERS, 10 BALLS, NET

One player serves from midcourt. Two players alternate passing to a setter who sets for the passer to lob spike over the net to the server. Rotate positions after 10 successful lob spikes. Other players chase balls.

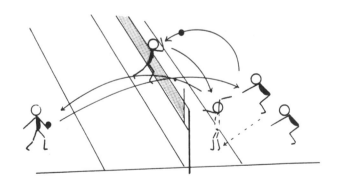

**WHO SET THE BALL
WHEN YOU SCORED.**

GAME 183
FOREARM PASS, SET, 4 PLAYERS,
1 BALL, NET

Two players on each team and the court split in half. One player plays back court and serves or passes. One player plays front court and sets. Serve to start play. The ball is passed, set and overhand passed over the net to the back-court player as play continues. Rotate positions with change of serve.

Start by co-operating with your opponents and try to make 10 successful passes over the net without a mistake. Next, force the back row player to move further and further to make the pass. Next, use a lob spike rather than an overhand pass over the net.

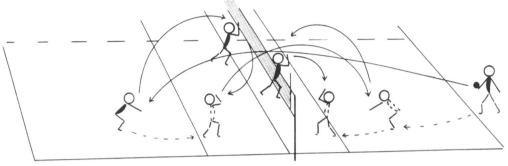

OBJECTIVE
To improve tipping skills

DRILL 184
TIP, 2 PLAYERS, 1 BALL

One player tosses the ball up, jumps and tips to the other player who catches the ball, tosses it up, jumps and tips it back. Gradually move further apart.

DRILL 185
TIP, 2 PLAYERS, 1 BALL

One player tosses the ball up to the other player who jumps and tips the ball back. Start close together and gradually move further apart.

GAME 186
TIP, 2 PLAYERS, 1 BALL, NET

One player tosses the ball over the net and the other player tips to an open space. The tosser must move to dig the ball. The tosser scores if the ball is passed reasonably. The tipper scores if the tipped ball is not passed. Alternate tossers.

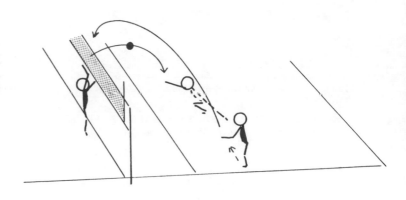

DRILL 187
TIP, 3 PLAYERS, 2 BALLS, NET

One player tosses the ball for the attacker to tip over the net to the third player who acts as a target. The target player catches the ball and rolls it back to the tosser. Both the tosser and the target player start with a ball. As soon as the tosser throws the first ball up, the target player rolls the second ball to the tosser. Keep going as rapidly as possible. Have the target player move each time.

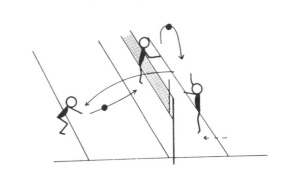

DRILL 188
TIP, DIG, 3 PLAYERS, 1 BALL, NET

One player tosses for the second player to tip to score. The third player on the other side of the net attempts to dig the tip. Tip from all three front-row positions. Have the defensive player play each of the three back-court positions and tip to the appropriate area of responsibility. Set goals and rotate once the goals are reached.

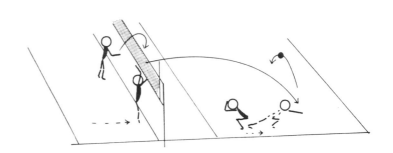

DRILL 189
TIP, PASS, SET, 3 PLAYERS, 2 BALLS, NET

One player tosses or serves a ball over the net to the attacker who passes to the setter. The ball is set and the attacker tips to a target close to the tosser/server. Repeat as rapidly as the skill level permits.

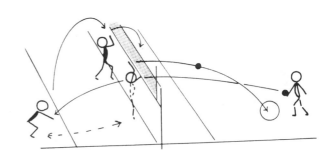

DRILL 190
TIP, SET, 3 PLAYERS, 1 BALL, NET

The attacker tosses the ball to the setter who sets for the attacker to tip. The defender on the other side moves forward or backward, to the left or right, as the ball is set. The attacker must tip away from the defender. Gradually have the defender delay moving until just before the ball is tipped.

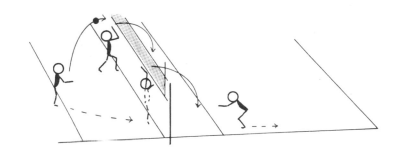

DRILL 191
TIP, 3 PLAYERS, 10 BALLS, NET

One player serves or throws the ball over the net to the attacker who passes to the setter. The ball is set and the attacker tips to an open place on the court. The server must anticipate the tip and move in to catch the ball and then, as quickly as possible, serve or throw the ball over the net for the attacker to pass again.

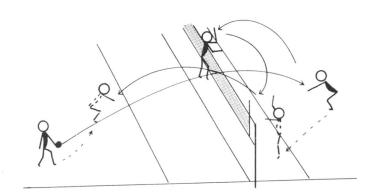

DRILL 192
TIP, PASS, SET, 3 PLAYERS, 2 BALLS, NET

One player tosses a ball over the net to the attacker who passes to the setter and then moves in to tip. The attacker and setter switch positions. The tosser then throws a second ball over the net for the setter to pass and then tip while the first attacker sets. Continue as rapidly as possible. Tip directly to the tosser.

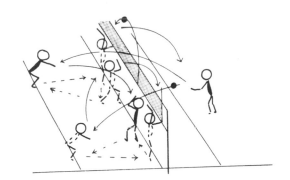

DRILL 193
TIP, PASS, SET, 4 PLAYERS, 1 BALL, NET

Two players on each side of the net. One player starts the drill by tossing a ball over the net for the other two players to pass, set and tip. The two teams try to keep that ball in play as long as possible without an error. Set a goal of 5 to 10 times over the net with a pass, set and tip on each side. Start within a confined court space and gradually make the space bigger for more skilled players.

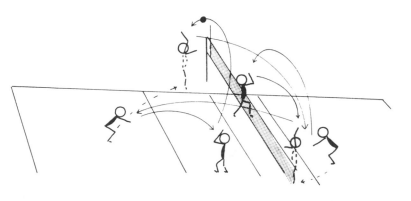

DRILL 194
TIP, SET, DIG, 8-10 PLAYERS,
10 BALLS, NET

One player tosses balls to a setter. Two players alternate tipping and two players alternate digging on the other side of the net. Toss and tip as rapidly as possible to force both the attackers and the defensive players to recover quickly. The other players chase balls and feed them to the tosser.

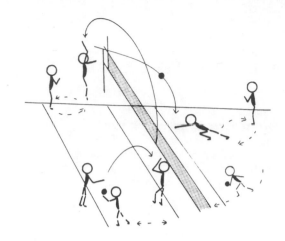

GAME 195
TIP, SET, 8-10 PLAYERS,
8 BALLS, NET, 9 HOOPS/CHAIRS

GOLF. Place the hoops or chairs around the court and number the targets (holes) from 1 to 9. Each player in turn tosses a ball to the setter and tries to tip to each of the 9 targets in proper rotation. Keep score on the number of attempts at each target (hole) and the total for 9 holes. For the back nine, tip from the other side of the court in reverse order.

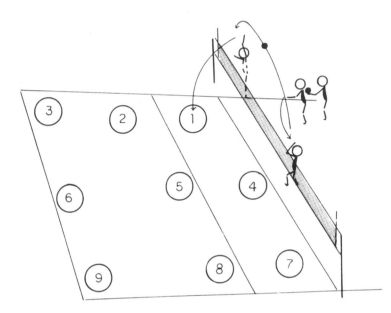

GAME 196
TIP, DIG, 6-12 PLAYERS, 1 BALL,
NET

Start with teams of 3 to 6 players on each side of the net. The object is to pass, set and tip with no spiking. Point or side-out is scored when a team is unable to return the ball over the net. Modifications to the game can be made according to the skill level of the players. For lower level players, instead of serving from behind the end line, serve from behind the attack line. If you have only 3 players, decrease the size of the court. To force the players to control the pass and set, count as an error any ball that is not tipped over the net. For beginners, allow a minimum of 3 contacts and a maximum of 4 contacts to allow for a decent set.

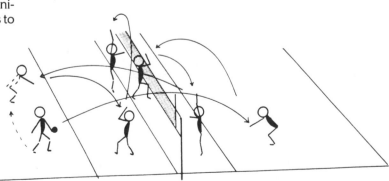

OBJECTIVE
To develop the ability to spike past the block

DRILL 197
SPIKE, 5 PLAYERS, NET, 5 TENNIS BALLS, 1 CHAIR

The chair is placed as a target on the other side of the net. The players approach, jump and throw the ball over the net at the target. Throw from all front-row positions and change the positions of the target chair to force the player to throw both straight as well as sharp cross-court.

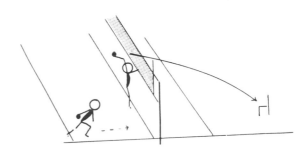

DRILL 198
SPIKE, 5 PLAYERS, 15 BALLS, NET, 1 CHAIR

One player tosses balls close to the net and two attackers alternate spiking at the target chair. The other players chase and feed balls to the tosser. Hit from all front row positions. Change the positions of the target chair. Attempt to hit straight down the line or sharp cross-court.

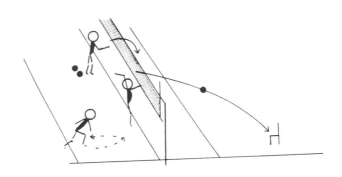

DRILL 199
SPIKE, 5 PLAYERS, 15 BALLS, NET, 2 CHAIRS

The chairs are placed on the attack line at each side of the court. One player tosses balls for two players who alternate spiking. As the player starts to jump, the tosser yells "line" or "cross-court", and the spiker must aim at the appropriate chair. Gradually delay shouting instructions thus giving the spiker less time to react.

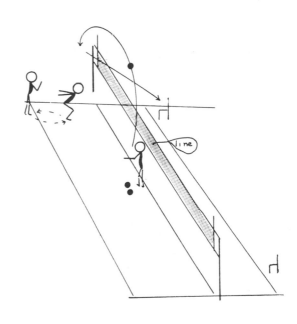

DRILL 200
SPIKE, 6 PLAYERS, 20 BALLS, NET, BLOCKING BOARD

One player holds the blocking board and moves it to the left or right as the spiker starts to jump. One player tosses balls for two players to alternate spiking. The spiker must hit to avoid the blocking board. The other players chase balls and feed them to the tosser.

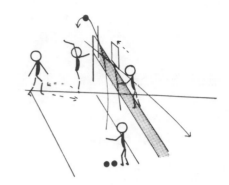

DRILL 201
SPIKE, 7 PLAYERS, 10 BALLS, NET

One player tosses balls continuously for the attacker to spike. One player blocks, first to protect one direction and second to protect the other direction, thus shifting the block left or right. The spiker must hit to avoid the block by alternating directions with each hit. The other players chase balls and feed them to the tosser.

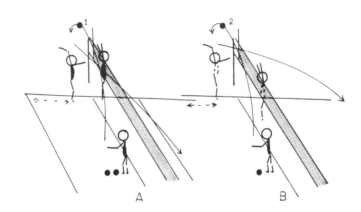

DRILL 202
SPIKE, 9 PLAYERS, 20 BALLS, NET

One player tosses balls for two players to alternate spiking. Two players block and set the block so as to protect the line or cross-court. The spiker must hit to avoid the block. Start by setting the block early and then gradually delay setting the block to give the hitter less time to adjust. The other players chase balls and feed them to the tosser. Attack and block from all front row positions.

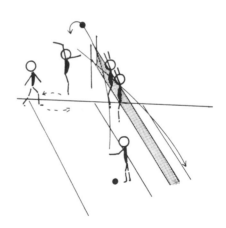

GAME 203
SPIKE, BLOCK, 7 PLAYERS, 20 BALLS, NET

Two players on opposite sides of the net alternate spiking and blocking. Two tossers alternate throwing balls up to the attacker on their side of the net while the opponent blocks. The other player chase balls and feed them to the tosser. Score 1 point each time the hit is in and 2 points for a block. Play to 5 or 7 points and change teams.

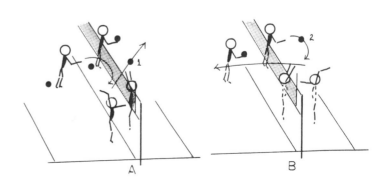

DRILL 204
SPIKE, 7 PLAYERS, 20 BALLS, NET

One player tosses for two players to alternate spiking while two players block. The blockers start, by leaving a hole between them in the block and the attacker must spike through the hole in the block. The other players chase balls and feed them to the tosser. Hit from all front row positions.

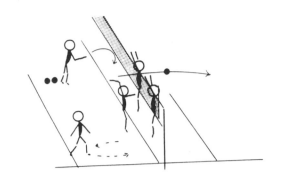

DRILL 205
SPIKE, 7 PLAYERS, 20 BALLS, NET

One player tosses for two players to alternate spiking while two players block. The blockers randomly block the line, cross-court, or leave a hole in the block. The spiker must hit to avoid the block or hit through the hole in the block. The other players chase balls and feed them to the tosser. Hit from all front row positions.

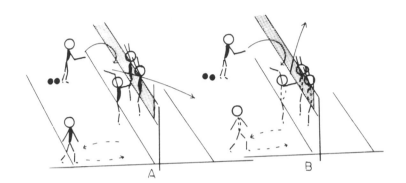

OBJECTIVE
To develop setting and spiking
skills

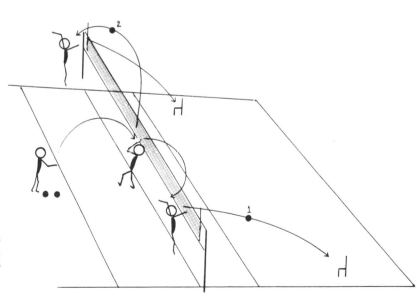

DRILL 206
SET AND SPIKE, 4 PLAYERS, 10 BALLS, NET, 2 CHAIRS

One player tosses the ball to the setter who alternates setting forward and backward to two hitters who attempt to spike the ball at the chairs. Spike line and move the position of the chairs either closer to or away from the net.

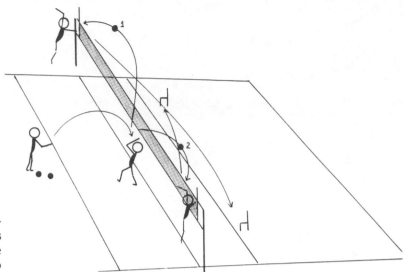

DRILL 207
SET AND SPIKE, 4 PLAYERS,
10 BALLS, NET, 2 CHAIRS

One player tosses the ball to the setter who alternates setting forward and backward to two hitters
who attempt to spike the ball at the chairs. Spike
cross-court and gradually move the chairs closer to
the net.

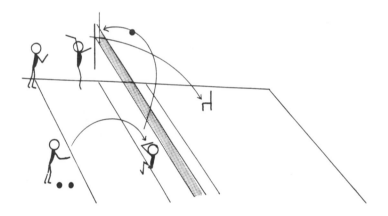

DRILL 208
SET AND SPIKE, 4 PLAYERS,
10 BALLS, NET, 1 CHAIR

One player tosses the ball to the setter so that the
setter must squat low to set. The ball is set forward
to 2 hitters who alternate spiking at the chair. Set
the chair up either for a line or cross-court attack.

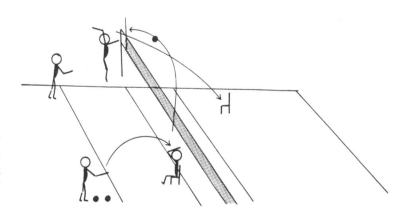

DRILL 209
SET AND SPIKE, 4 PLAYERS,
10 BALLS, NET, 2 CHAIRS

One player tosses the ball to the setter. The setter
sits on the chair and sets from a sitting position to
two hitters who alternate spiking at the other target
chair. The purpose of this drill is to develop finger
and wrist action, and control while setting.

DRILL 210
SET AND SPIKE, 4 PLAYERS,
10 BALLS, NET, 1 CHAIR

One player tosses the ball above and close to the net forcing the setter to jump and set forward to two hitters who alternate spiking at the target chair.

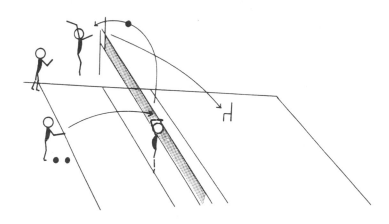

DRILL 211
SET AND SPIKE, 4 PLAYERS,
10 BALLS, NET, 1 CHAIR

One player tosses the ball above and close to the net forcing the setter to jump and set backward to two hitters who alternate spiking at the target chair.

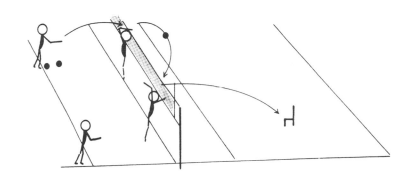

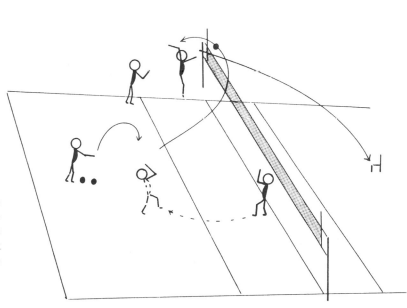

DRILL 212
SET AND SPIKE, 4 PLAYERS,
10 BALLS, NET, 1 CHAIR

One player tosses the ball up forcing the setter to run and set the ball forward to two hitters who alternate spiking at the target chair. Make the toss as difficult as the setter's skills permit. The spikers must attempt to hit the target chair each time, even if the set is bad. Do the same drill with a backward set.

OBJECTIVE
To teach the player to position the block

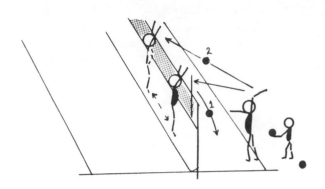

DRILL 213
BLOCK, 3 PLAYERS, 10 BALLS, NET

One player stands about 2 metres back from the net and lob spikes the ball alternately down the line or cross-court. The blocker must read and shift to block. A third player feeds balls to the spiker.

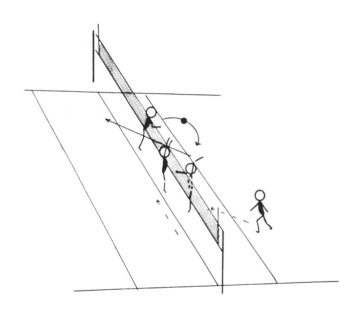

DRILL 214
BLOCK, 3 PLAYERS, 10 BALLS, NET

One player tosses the ball for a player to spike. The spiker must approach along a straight line and hit in the direction of their approach. Hit both line and cross-court. Do this drill from both sides and the middle of the net.

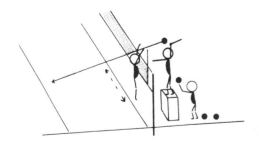

DRILL 215
BLOCK, 3 PLAYERS, 10 BALLS, NET, PLATFORM

One player stands on a spiking platform and adjusts the shoulders before hitting to indicate if they will hit cross-court or line. The spiker then hits in that direction. The blocker adjusts the position of the block accordingly. Do this drill from both sides and the middle of the net.

DRILL 216
BLOCK, 4 PLAYERS, 10 BALLS, NET

One player tosses to 2 players who alternate spiking from one side and the middle. They must always hit in the same direction, either line or cross-court. The blocker must shift and block each spiker. Start slowly to allow the blocker time to think and gradually speed up the drill.

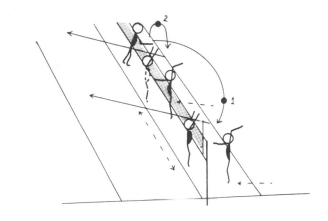

DRILL 217
BLOCK, 6 PLAYERS, 10 BALLS, NET

One player is fed balls and tosses to 3 players who alternate spiking from left, middle and right. They must always hit in the same direction, either line or cross-court. The blocker must shift and block each spiker. Allow the blocker enough time to recover, think and position correctly.

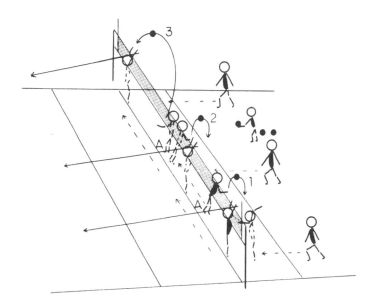

DRILL 218
BLOCK, 6 PLAYERS, 10 BALLS, NET

Three attackers hit from left, middle and right. One player tosses the ball alternately to each attacker. The players must hit either line or cross-court but must hit in the direction of the approach. The blocker must shift and block each spiker. Allow the blocker enough time to recover, think and position correctly.

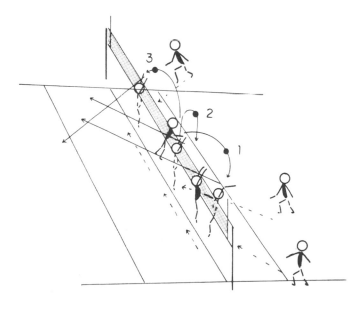

DRILL 219
BLOCK, 6 PLAYERS, 10 BALLS, NET

Three players attack from left, middle and right. One player tosses the balls to the setter who alternates setting to each spiker. The attackers must hit in the direction of their approach and may change their approach each time they hit. The blocker must read the approach and anticipate the direction of the attack. The blocker shifts to block all three positions. Allow the blocker enough time to recover, think and position correctly.

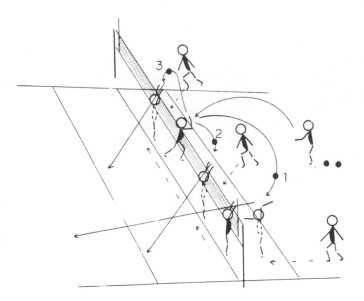

DRILL 220
BLOCK, 7 PLAYERS, 10 BALLS, NET

Three players attack from left, middle and right. The ball is tossed over the net to a back row player who passes to the setter. The setter sets the ball high to any one of the attackers. The blocker must watch the pass and the setter and try to read the direction of the set. The attackers must hit in the direction of their approach. The blocker shifts to block all three positions.

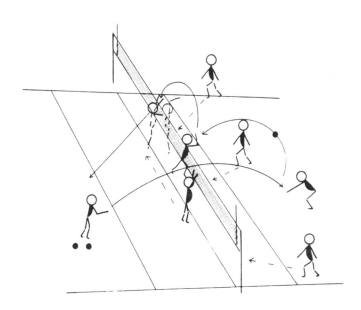

**EXTRA EFFORT
IS THE DIFFERENCE
BETWEEN AN AVERAGE
AND A GREAT ATHLETE.**

OBJECTIVE
To improve positioning and timing the block

DRILL 221
BLOCK, 2 PLAYERS, 1 BALL, NET

The attacker tosses the ball up high and close to the net, jumps and spikes the ball directly into the blocker's hands. The other player jumps and blocks.

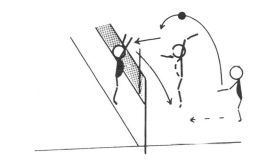

DRILL 222
BLOCK, 2 PLAYERS, 1 BALL, NET.

The attacker tosses the ball up 1 or more metres back from the net and spikes the ball cross-court. The blocker adjusts their position, jumps and blocks. Do the same down the line. The attacker must hit in the direction they are facing.

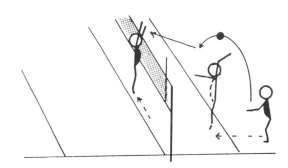

DRILL 223
BLOCK, 2 PLAYERS, 10 PLAYERS, NET

The attacker randomly tosses the ball high or low, close to the net or away from the net, and to various places along the net and spikes. The blocker must adjust the position and timing of the block.

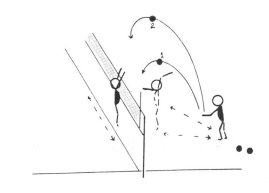

DRILL 224
BLOCK, 2 PLAYERS, 10 BALLS, NET

The blocker tosses the ball high over the net for the attacker to spike. The blocker then moves in to block. Have the blocker toss the ball from various angles and then move in to block. Be sure the blocker jumps straight up and does not drift forward.

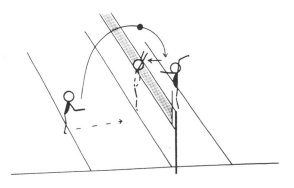

DRILL 225
BLOCK, 3 PLAYERS, 10 BALLS, NET

Two attackers alternately toss and spike. The blocker must shift and block each attacker. Start by having the attacker hit directly into the blocker's hands to help the player get the feel of blocking.

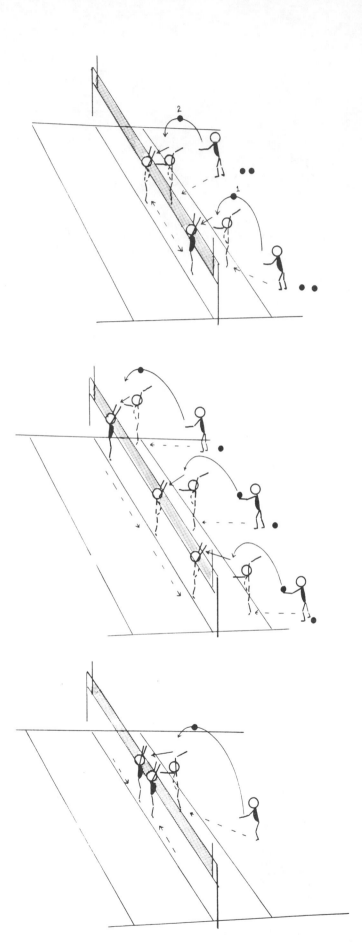

DRILL 226
BLOCK, 4 PLAYERS, 10 BALLS, NET

Three attackers alternately toss and spike from the side, middle and side. The blocker must shift and block each position. The attacker should hit directly into the blocker's hands. The blocker should try to press the ball back toward the middle of the court.

DRILL 227
BLOCK, 3 PLAYERS, 10 BALLS, NET

The attacker tosses the ball up high about one metre back from the net, jumps and spikes the ball directly into the block. Always hit in the same direction. The two blockers must synchronize their jump and try not to leave a hole in the block.

In this drill, have the outside player set the position and timing of the block. The middle player watches their teammate (not the ball or the attacker) and then closes on the partner to form the block.

Both blockers should press the ball back toward the middle of the court.

GAME 228
BLOCK, 3 PLAYERS, 1 BALL,
NET

Two blockers vs. one attacker. The attacker tosses the ball up to various places along the net, jumps and spikes. The blockers adjust and block. Score a point for the blockers if the block is successful and a point for the attacker if the ball is spiked into court. Rotate attackers after each game.

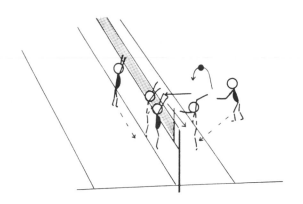

OBJECTIVE
**To teach players to position
and close the block**

DRILL 229
BLOCK, 3 PLAYERS, COACH,
10 BALLS, NET

Lower the height of the net so that the blockers can reach above the net without jumping. The coach tosses the ball up close to the net in front of the blockers. The attacker lob spikes the ball in a predetermined direction (i.e. line or cross-court) and the blockers move and block (no jump). Check to see that the blockers are lined up properly and that the hands are spread optimally. Do the same for each direction of attack and from each attack position. It may be necessary to first have the coach hold the ball up above the net and have the blockers line up to block, and to also have the blockers adjust for the line or cross-court attack.

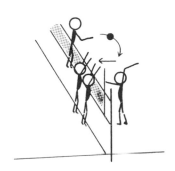

DRILL 230
BLOCK, 3 PLAYERS, COACH,
10 BALLS, NET

Same as the previous drill except that the blockers now start in their respective front row positions and shift to close the block.

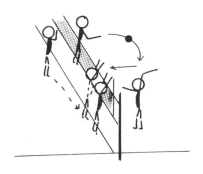

DRILL 231
BLOCK, 3 PLAYERS, COACH,
10 BALLS, NET

The net is at regulation height or slightly low. The coach tosses the ball up close to the net in front of the blockers for the attacker to hit in a predetermined direction (i.e., line or cross-court). The blockers move, jump and block. Check to see that the blockers shift or move to the proper place in front of the spiker and that the hands are in the proper position. Do the same for each direction of attack and from each of the attack positions.

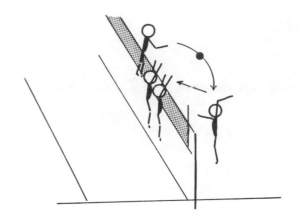

DRILL 232
BLOCK, 3 PLAYERS, COACH,
10 BALLS, NET

Same as the previous drill except that the blockers start in their respective front row positions and shift to close the block.

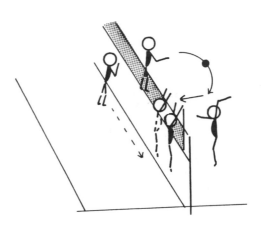

DRILL 233
BLOCK, 6-8 PLAYERS, 10 BALLS,
NET

One player alternates tossing to spikers at positions #2 and #4. The middle blocker on the other side shifts and blocks with the outside blockers at both sides putting up a two player block. Start with high throws to allow the blocker time to shift. Always hit in a predetermined direction. Extra players chase balls and feed them to the tosser.

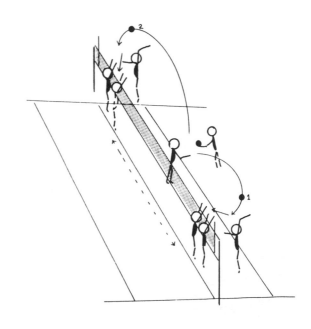

OBJECTIVE
To learn to recover a ball from the net

DRILL 234
NET RECOVERY, 1 PLAYER, 1 BALL, NET

The player tosses or spikes a ball into the net and digs the rebound high. Learn to crouch low, play the ball close to the floor, and pass it high. The player should have their side to the net. Throw from various angles, at various speeds and into different heights in the net.

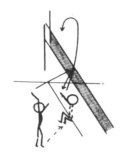

DRILL 235
NET RECOVERY, 2 PLAYERS, 1 BALL, NET

One player starts about 1 metre from the net and recovers a ball thrown into the net from various angles by the other player. Throw from both sides of the player.

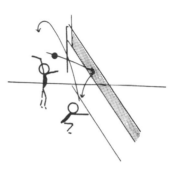

DRILL 236
NET RECOVERY, 2 PLAYERS, 1 BALL, NET

One player jumps to block. As the player lands, a second player throws a ball into the net. The blocker should squat low when landing and pass the ball high. Throw to both sides, from various angles and at varying speeds.

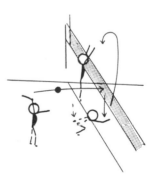

DRILL 237
NET RECOVERY, 2 PLAYERS, NET, CHAIR

One player stands on a chair and holds a ball above the net. The other player jumps to block the ball. As the blocker descends, the ball is dropped down in front of the blocker for them to pass high.

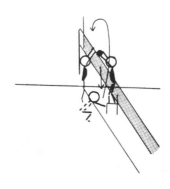

DRILL 238
NET RECOVERY, 2 PLAYERS, NET, CHAIR

One player stands on a chair and spikes the ball into the block so that the ball is driven down between the blocker and the net. The blocker will have to block slightly back from the net to make this easier. The blocker lands, crouches low and digs the ball high.

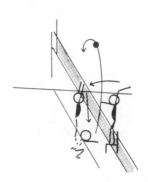

OBJECTIVE
To teach players to anticipate
their defensive positions
in reaction to the position
of the ball

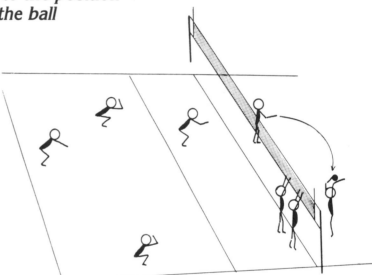

DRILL 239
DEFENSE, 7-9 PLAYERS, COACH, 1 BALL, NET

The coach tosses a ball to one of the front-row attackers. The defensive players on the other side move to assume their defensive positions as the attacker catches the ball. Emphasize proper body posture both with the blockers at the net as well as with the back-court players. Start with a high toss to the attacker and gradually lower the height so that the players have less time to respond and move into position. Blockers do not block but merely move to set up positions in front of the attacker.

DRILL 240
DEFENSE, 7-9 PLAYERS, COACH, 1 BALL, NET

The coach tosses the ball to one of the front row attackers but tosses the ball either close to or tight on the net, or further back from the net. The attacker catches the ball. The back-court defensive players move in closer to the net if the toss is close to the net and further back from the net if the toss is back from the net. Blockers do not block.

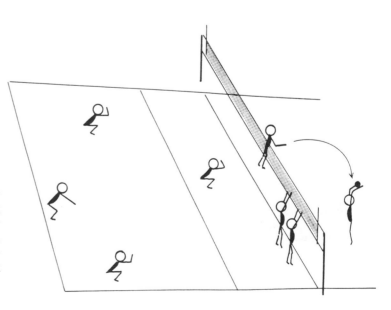

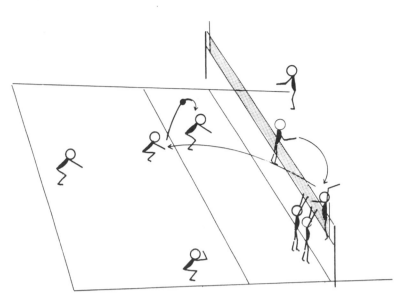

DRILL 241
DEFENSE, 7-9 PLAYERS, COACH,
1 BALL, NET

The coach tosses the ball to one of the front-row attackers at different distances back from the net. The attackers spike trying to avoid the block and the defensive players move to their positions and try to dig the ball. Emphasize moving to the right place on the court with the appropriate low posture in the back court. Start with high tosses to give the players time to think and respond and gradually lower the height of the toss.

OBJECTIVE
To teach players to anticipate their defensive positions in reaction to the actions of the attacker

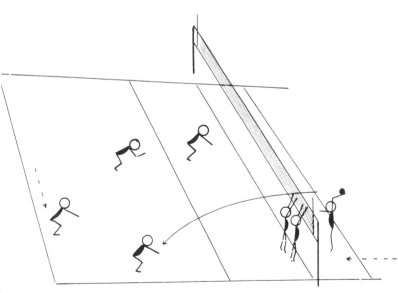

DRILL 242
DEFENSE, 7 PLAYERS, 1 BALL,
NET

An attacker approaches the net along a line, jumps and throws the ball over the net in the same direction as the approach, simulating a spike. The defensive players read the approach, anticipate the direction of the throw and move to dig the ball. The blockers do not jump to block.

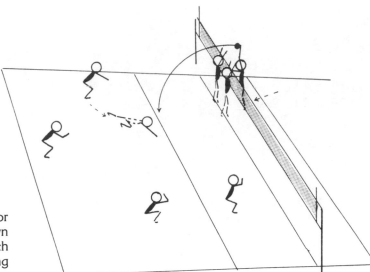

DRILL 243
DEFENSE, 7 PLAYERS, 1 BALL, NET

An attacker approaches the net at either a slow or fast speed. If the approach is slow, the ball is thrown softly over the net simulating a tip. If the approach is fast, the ball is thrown fast over the net simulating a spike. The blockers do not jump to block.

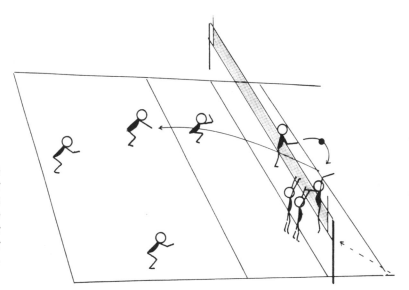

DRILL 244
DEFENSE, 7 PLAYERS, 1 BALL, NET

The coach tosses the ball for an attacker to hit. The attacker must attack in the same direction as their approach. Have the attacker do several attacks in a row in the same direction (e.g., line). Once the defense has learned to read the attack, have the attacker change and hit in a new direction from another place, from close to the net or back from the net. The blockers do not jump to block.

ANTICIPATION
MAKES FOR
POSITION.

OBJECTIVE
To teach players to anticipate
their defensive positions in
reaction to the responses of
their teammates

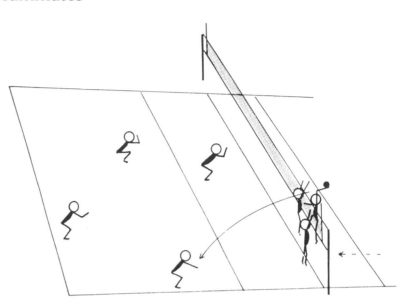

DRILL 245 DEFENSE, 7 PLAYERS, 1 BALL, NET

The attacker runs in, jumps and throws the ball over the net. The blockers now jump to block and the coach instructs the blockers to set the block to stop the line attack or the angle attack, to jump late, to leave a hole in the block, not to jump, or for only one blocker to jump. The attacker then throws the ball past the block, through the block, or over the blockers in the appropriate direction forcing the back row players to react appropriately to dig the ball.

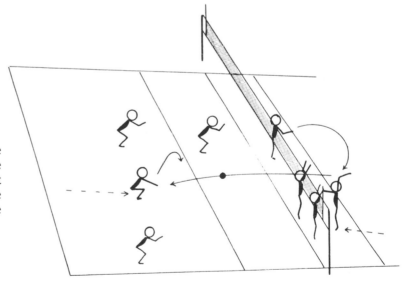

DRILL 246
DEFENSE, 7 PLAYERS, COACH, 1 BALL, NET

The coach tosses a ball for an attacker to spike. The coach instructs the blockers to leave a hole in the block, to block line or cross-court, to jump late, not to block, or puts a short player in to block. The back-court defensive players must learn to read the block and react accordingly.

With the previous drills, have the players respond verbally as well as physically so that the coach can tell if the player has perceived the situation correctly. This also helps force the player to think and respond.

The defensive players must learn to react to the ball, learn to read the attacker, and learn to respond to the actions of the blockers. Start with individual reactions to simple combinations and gradually move to more complex combinations.

NOTES

PART IV

INTERMEDIATE AND

ADVANCED DRILLS

OBJECTIVE
To improve passing skills

DRILL 247
PASS, 2 PLAYERS, 1 BALL, WALL OR NET

Two players stand facing the wall or net and about 1 metre away from the wall. The players pass the ball sideways without touching the wall. Try the same drill with a jump set at the net. Try the same drill from a crouched position.

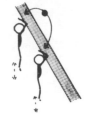

DRILL 248
PASS, 3 PLAYERS, 1 BALL, NET

One player starts at the net and passes the ball straight up and then moves out. The other two players start beyond the attack line. The second player moves in under the pass and sets it straight up for the next player in line to move in and pass. Keep passing the ball straight up and rotating positions. The same drill can be done with a different angle of approach and also with a jump set or a squat set.

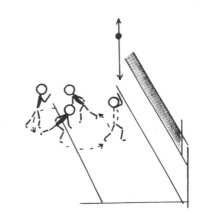

DRILL 249
PASS, 4 PLAYERS, 1 BALL, NET

Two players start on each side of the net beyond the attack line. The ball is passed back and forth over the net. The players move to the back of their own line after passing. The players can also cross under the net to the end of the other line after passing. Do the same with jump sets, with short passes or with one arm digs.

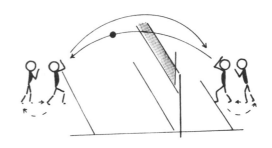

DRILL 250
PASS, 3 PLAYERS, 1 BALL, NET

One player on one side of the net and two players on the other side of the net with a ball. The first player sets the ball over the net and moves under the net to take the position of the person to whom the pass was made. The ball is passed back and forth over the net with the player moving after the ball. Do this same drill with jump sets. The same drill can be done beside the net with jump sets.

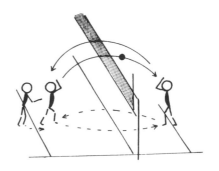

DRILL 251
PASS, 6 PLAYERS, 1 BALL, NET

Three players start on each side of the net. One player on each side starts at the net and the other two players start beyond the attack line. The ball is passed from a back player to the front player who sets or bumps the ball backward over the net to the back player on the other side who passes to the front player on that side. Continue. The player follows the pass and takes the position of the player to whom the pass was made.

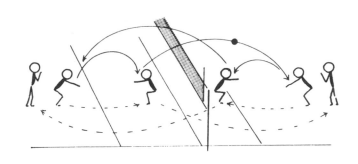

GAME 252
PASS, 4 PLAYERS, 1 BALL, NET

Cut the court in half from back line to back line. Two players on each side. The ball is passed from the back player to the front player who must pass the ball backward over the net beyond the attack line. The front and back players exchange places after passing the ball over the net. Score a point or side out each time the ball is not passed over the net or if it is passed out of court. Do with the forearm pass only, the overhand pass only, or a mixture of both passes.

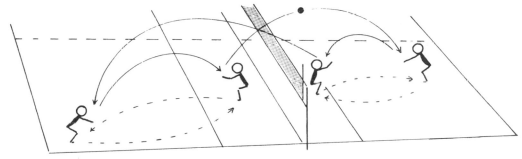

DRILL 253
PASS, 2 PLAYERS, 1 BALL, COURT

Two players start in diagonally opposite corners of the court and pass back and forth. The player in the back corner should try to make a perfect set to the net.

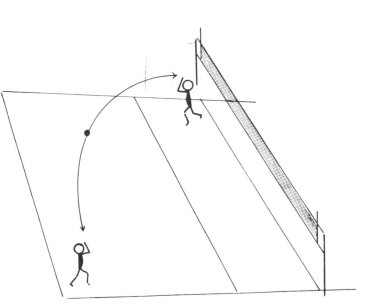

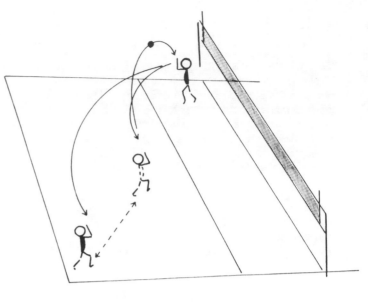

DRILL 254
PASS, 2 PLAYERS, 1 BALL, COURT

Two players start in diagonally opposite corners of the court. The player near the net stays stationary and passes first to mid-court and then to the back corner. The other player must move forward and backward to make each pass. The moving player must try to make a perfect set to the net.

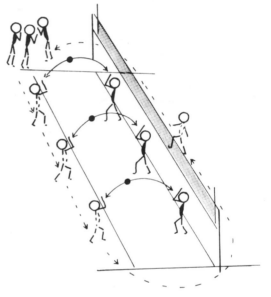

DRILL 255
PASS, 8-12 PLAYERS, 3 BALLS, NET

Three players start along the net each with a ball. The other players start beyond the attack line at one side line. Each player moves sideways across the court and passes the ball back to the player at the net. Keep moving continuously and try to keep the rhythm even. The moving players go back to the end of the line.

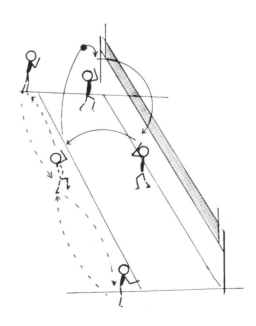

DRILL 256
PASS, 4 PLAYERS, 2 BALLS, NET

Two players start at the net, one in position #4 and the other in position #3. Two players start beyond the attack line and outside the sideline, one on each side. The player in position #3 passes the ball to mid court and one player moves in from the side line and passes to the player in position #4. The player in position #4 passes to position #3 and #3 passes for the second player to move in and pass to position #4. Once the concept of the drill is mastered, use two balls and keep both balls going. Try to make a perfect set to position #4 or also set to position #2.

DRILL 257
PASS, 3 PLAYERS, 1 BALL, NET

Two players start at the net in positions #2 and #3. One player starts beyond the back line. The player in position #2 passes the ball to the mid-court area. The back-line player must move in under the ball and pass it to the player in position #3, and then move back beyond the back line and move in to make the next pass. Keep the ball going continuously and repeat until the back-line player fatigues and then rotate.

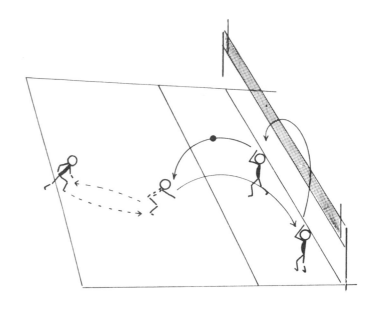

DRILL 258
PASS, SET, 3 PLAYERS, 1 BALL, NET, PLATFORM

One player stands on a platform on the other side of the net. (A) The platform player tips or spikes a ball at a back-court player who passes to a setter. (B) The setter then sets to the platform player who holds the arms over the net as a target and catches the ball.

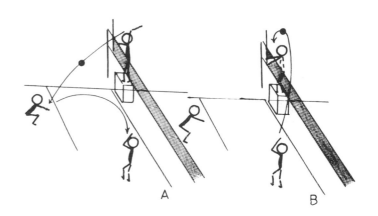

DRILL 259
PASS, 3 PLAYERS, 1 BALL, NET

Two players start in the front corners of the court and one player starts in one of the back corners. The ball is passed diagonally from the back to the front, across the front and again to the back. Have the back player change corners and reverse the direction of the pass. Rotate positions.

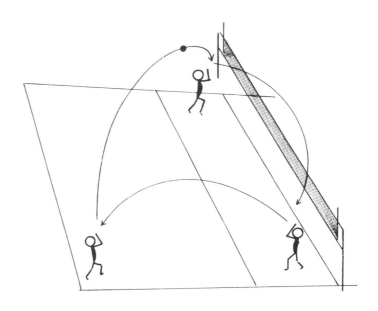

DRILL 260
PASS, 3 PLAYERS, 2 BALLS, NET

Two players start in the front corners of the court and one player starts in one of the back corners. One of the front players passes diagonally to the back corner. The back player must run across court and pass the ball back. Then the other front player passes to the other back corner and the back player again runs and passes the ball back. Keep the back-court player running. The front players will have to catch the ball and then toss to pass to allow the player time to move. Rotate when the player fatigues.

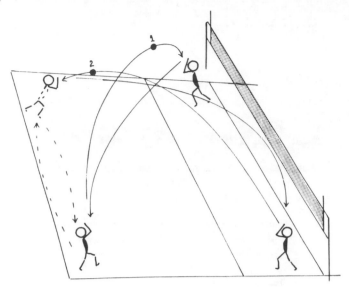

DRILL 261
PASS, 3 PLAYERS, 1 BALL, NET

Two players start in the front corners of the court. One player starts in one back corner. A front player passes a ball diagonally to the back corner and the back player must move across court and pass the ball straight ahead to the other front player who then passes diagonally to the other back corner. The back player runs across court and again passes straight ahead to the first front player. Continue and rotate when the player fatigues. Shorten the distance for less skilled players.

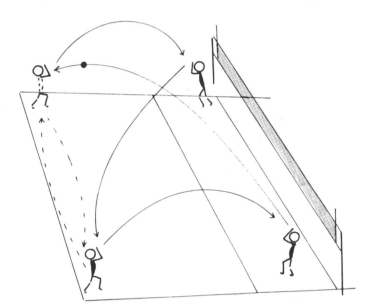

DRILL 262
PASS, 4 PLAYERS, 1 BALL, NET

Two players start at each sideline. The ball is passed back and forth along the net. The players jump to block, land and pass and then move back while the partner does the same. Do the drill with both the overhand pass and the forearm pass. Advanced players can do it with a jump set. Have one side use a forearm pass while the other passes high. Set goals of 50 passes in a row without an error.

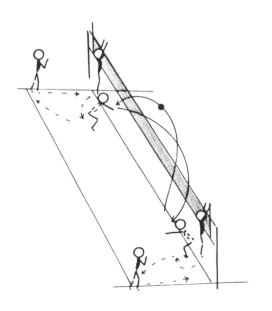

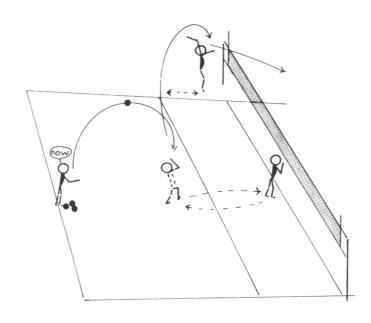

DRILL 263
PASS, 3 PLAYERS, 10 BALLS,
NET

One player starts at the net. A tosser stands at the back line and tosses a ball up high to the mid-court area. As the ball is thrown, the tosser yells "now" and the player must turn, find the ball, run and set it to a target player at the net. The target player can also spike the set. A variation is to have the player jump to block and as the blocker lands, the ball is tossed for the player to turn and run and pass.

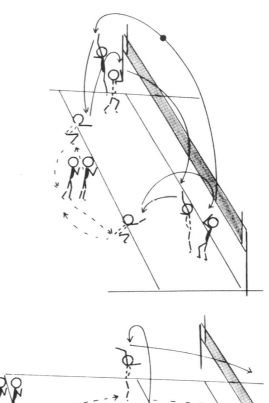

DRILL 264
PASS, COVER, TIP, 4-6 PLAYERS,
1 BALL, NET

One tipper starts in each of the front corners near the net. The other players start in a line in mid-court beyond the attack line. One tipper starts the drill by setting to the other front row tipper. The first player in line moves in to cover and the front-row player tips the ball for the digger to pass up to the tipper. The tipper then passes across court to the other tipper while the second player in line moves in to cover and the ball is tipped and passed. Continue.

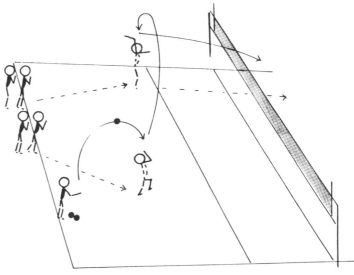

DRILL 265
PASS, SPIKE, 6-12 PLAYERS,
20 BALLS, NET

One player starts at the back line and tosses balls to the mid-court area. The other players line up in two lines behind the back line. One of the players moves forward and sets the ball high to the other player to move in for a back-court attack. Chase the ball, return it to the tosser and move to the end of the other line. This same drill can be done with the two players starting at the net and having to move backward to make the set and attack. They could also cross.

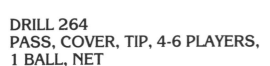

OBJECTIVE
To develop ability to pass balls that are tipped

DRILL 266
TIP DIG, 2 PLAYERS, 1 BALL, NET

One player stands at the net holding the ball high above the head. They toss the ball to a place in front of the defensive player (who is waiting beyond the attack line in a low defensive stance) forcing that player to crouch low and dig the ball back up to the partner at the net. Toss the ball to each side of the defensive player. Gradually make it more difficult by forcing the defensive player to start from further back and force the player to dive or roll to dig the ball.

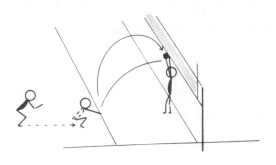

DRILL 267
TIP DIG, 2 PLAYERS, 1 BALL, NET

The defensive player starts about mid-court in a low defensive stance. The other player stands close to the net, tosses the ball up, jumps and tips it to the defensive player who digs the ball up high back to the partner.

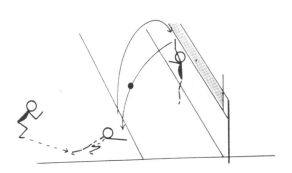

DRILL 268
TIP DIG, 2 PLAYERS, 1 BALL, NET

The defensive player starts beyond mid-court in a low defensive stance. The other player stands close to the net, tosses the ball up, jumps and either tips or hits the ball at half speed to the defensive player. The defensive player must take a cue from the arm action of the attacker to read if the ball will be tipped or spiked, and dig the ball up high to their partner.

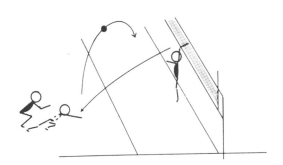

DRILL 269
TIP DIG, 4 PLAYERS, 1 BALL, NET

The defensive player starts beyond mid-court in a low defensive stance. One player stands close to the net as a target receiver. On the other side of the net, one player tosses or sets the ball for the attacker to tip towards the defensive player. The defensive player attempts to dig the ball up to the target player.

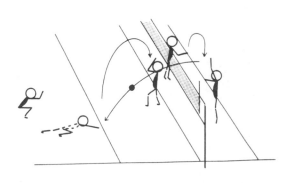

DRILL 270
TIP DIG, 4 PLAYERS, 1 BALL, NET

The defensive player starts beyond mid-court in a low defensive stance. One player starts close to the net as a blocker and then as a target receiver. On the other side of the net, one player tosses or sets the ball for the attacker to tip towards the defensive player over top of the blocker. The defensive player attempts to dig the ball up to a target area, preferably the setting place, as the blocker moves to that target area to receive the tip recovery. Have the attacker spike the ball on occasion. Have the blocker call as they move to the target area.

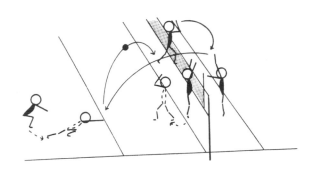

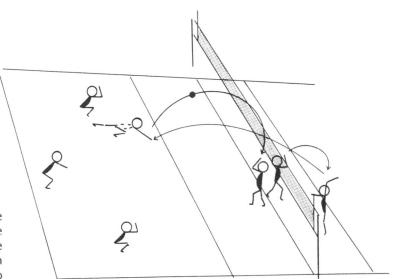

DRILL 271
TIP DIG, 6 PLAYERS, 10 BALLS, NET

Three players start in the three back-court defensive positions. One player stands close to the net in the setting place as a target. On the other side of the net, one player sets and one player tips in random order to any of the three defensive players who attempt to dig the ball up to the target player. Gradually tip to make it more difficult to recover. Tip from all places along the net and occasionally spike on the attack.

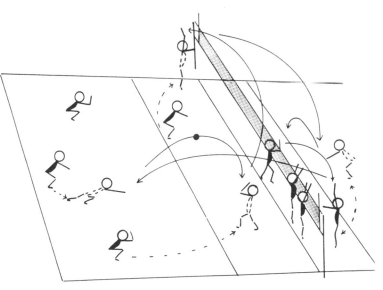

DRILL 272
TIP DIG, 8 PLAYERS, 10 BALLS, NET

Three players start in the three back-court defensive positions. Three other players start as blockers at the net. On the other side of the net, one player sets and one player tips in random order to any of the three defensive players who attempt to dig the ball up to the target area. As the ball is dug, one of the other back-court players moves under the ball and sets it to one of the front-row players to tip back to the attacker. If possible, the attacker passes the ball to the setter and continues the drill.

OBJECTIVE
To develop defensive reactions and skills

DRILL 273
DIG, 2 PLAYERS, 2 BALLS, WALL

One player serves against the wall. A second player starts behind the server and moves to dig the ball. The extra players chase balls and feed them to the server.

DRILL 274
DIG, 2 PLAYERS, 1 BALL, WALL

One player serves, throws, or spikes against the wall. The other player starts in front of the attacker and moves to dig the ball. The attacker chases the ball and attacks again. Repeat. Change positions after 15 hits.

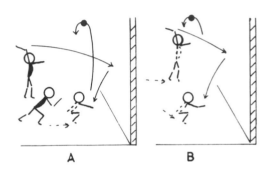

DRILL 275
DIG, 6 PLAYERS, 10 BALLS, WALL

Five players stand in a semi-circle around the digger who is positioned near the wall. Each attacker has two balls. The players spike or tip the ball in succession to the digger who attempts to pass the ball high back to the attacker. A variation is to have the spikers attack in random order.

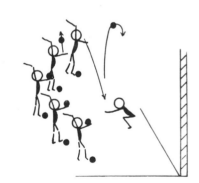

DRILL 276
PASS, DIG, 6-10 PLAYERS, COACH,
20 BALLS, NET, PLATFORM

The coach stands on the platform on the other side of the net and starts by tossing a "free ball" to the digger to pass to the setter at the net. The coach then spikes a ball at the digger to again be passed to the setter. Repeat with the next player in line. One player feeds balls to the coach and the extra players chase balls and feed them to the coach. Force the digger to move on the "free ball" and also the dig.

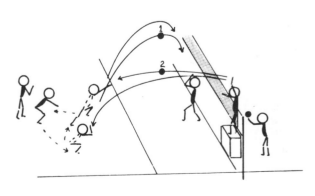

DRILL 277
DIG, 4 PLAYERS, COACH, 20 BALLS, NET, 2 PLATFORMS

The two platforms are placed side by side on the other side of the net. A coach and a player spike from the platforms. Two players alternate digging, first for a line spike and then move across court to dig a cross-court spike. A setter catches the balls that are dug. Two players feed balls to the hitters. Extra players chase balls.

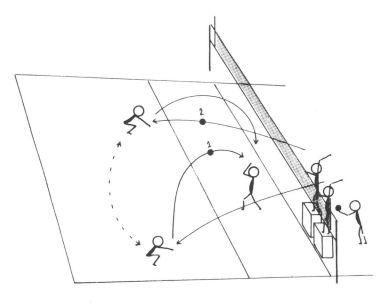

DRILL 278
DIG, 4 PLAYERS, COACH, 20 BALLS, NET, 2 PLATFORMS

The two platforms are placed side by side on the other side of the net. A coach spikes and a player tips from the platforms. Two players alternate digging to a setter. The coach spikes line for the digger to pass and the tipper tips cross-court for the digger to dive, and dig. Continue. Two players feed balls to the coach and tipper. Extra players chase balls.

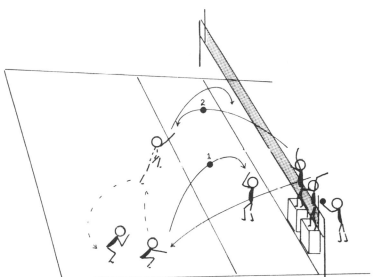

DRILL 279
DIG, 3 PLAYERS, COACH, 20 BALLS, NET, 2 PLATFORMS

The two platforms are placed on each side of the court on the other side of the net. A coach and a player alternate spiking from the platform at the digger who attempts to pass to a setter, first digging a line spike and then a cross-court spike. Two players feed balls to the coach and hitter. Extra players chase balls and feed them to the coach and hitter.

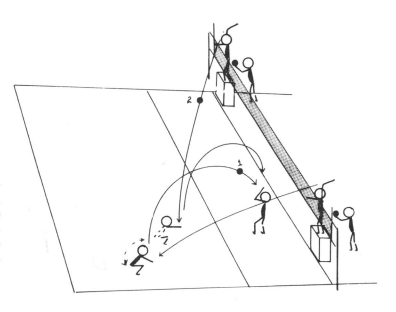

DRILL 280
DIG, ROLL, 3 PLAYERS, COACH,
10 BALLS

The coach starts about 5 metres in front of the players and tosses balls low alternately to the left and right of the player forcing the player to move, dig, and roll, first to the left and then to the right. Do as rapidly as the skill level will allow and toss low and to a point that will force the player to extend to the maximum. Dig the ball as high as possible. The other players chase balls and feed them to the coach.

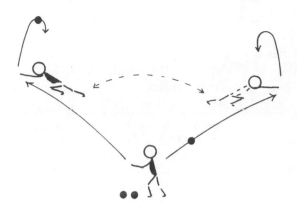

DRILL 281
DIG, SPIKE, SET, 3 PLAYERS,
10 BALLS, NET

One player tosses a ball to a setter who sets the ball high over the net and close to the net. The third player on the other side of the net jumps and spikes the ball back at the setter or the tosser who must dig the ball and then set it over the net again for the attacker to spike again. Continue.

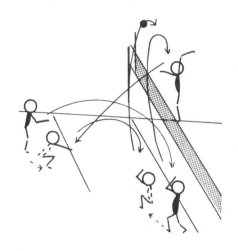

DRILL 282
DIG, SET, TIP, 3 PLAYERS,
10 BALLS, NET

One player tosses a ball to a setter who sets the ball over and close to the net. The third player on the other side of the net jumps and tips the ball back for either the setter or passer to dig and set over the net again. Continue.

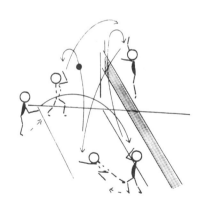

DRILL 283
DIG, SET, SPIKE, BLOCK,
3 PLAYERS, 10 BALLS, NET

(A) The attacker tosses a ball to a setter who sets and the attacker spikes while a third player blocks. (B) The setter will deliberately set some balls over the net and the blocker will spike. The attacker must then block and the setter must dig. The setter must move to recover any blocked balls.

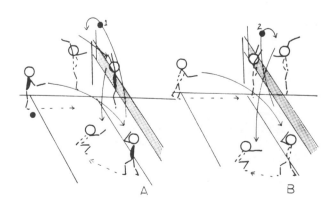

DRILL 284
DIG, PASS, SET, SPIKE,
4 PLAYERS, 10 BALLS, NET

Two players on each side of the net. (A) One player serves or tosses a ball over the net from mid-court and moves up to hit. The receiving players attempt to pass the ball over and close to the net for one of the two serving players to jump and spike directly back at one of the two receiving players. (B) The receiving players then dig, set and spike while the servers block. Repeat.

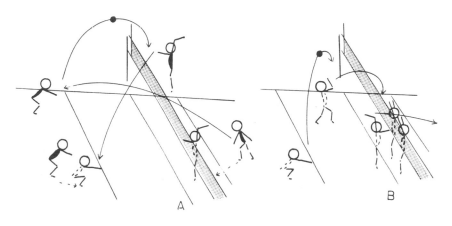

DRILL 285
DIG, SET, SPIKE, 9-12 PLAYERS,
10 BALLS, NET

Three players start playing defense in the three back-court positions. Two players start attacking from positions #2 and #4 on the other side of the net. A player tosses a ball to the setter who sets over the net to one of the attackers to spike or tip. The defensive players dig the ball to the setter who again sets over the net for an attacker to spike or tip. Continue. The tosser throws a new ball to the setter once a ball is dead. The extra players chase balls and feed them to the tosser. Rotate in groups of three.

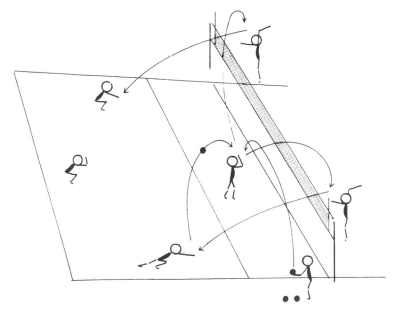

DRILL 286
DIG, BLOCK, SPIKE, SET,
8-10 PLAYERS, 20 BALLS, NET

Four players start on each side of the net, two of whom are tossers. (A) To start one tosser throws a ball up for a player to set and the other will spike. The opponents block. If the block is good, the attackers try to dig, set and spike again. If they fail to spike, a tosser on the other side throws a new ball in to be set, spiked and blocked. (B) If the ball is not blocked, however, a tosser on the side of the blockers tosses a ball to the side for one of the blockers to dive and dig, and the ball is set and spiked. If the blockers fail to dig, set and spike, a second ball is tossed forcing the blockers to dive and dig, set and spike again. This is repeated until the sequence results in a successful spike. (C) Continue the same for both sides. Extra players chase balls. Rotate in pairs.

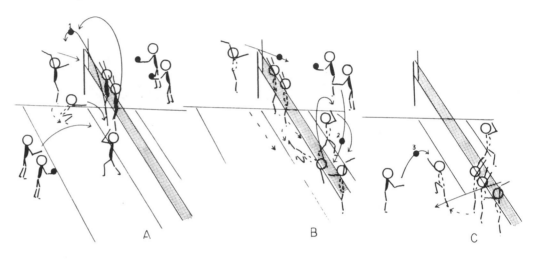

OBJECTIVE
To improve the ability to cover and dig a blocked ball

DRILL 287
BLOCK, COVER, 2 PLAYERS,
1 BALL, WALL

The spiker tosses a ball up, jumps and spikes at the wall. The other player moves in to cover and dig the rebound up high. Hit at varying speeds. The cover will be more realistic if the ball is spiked into a gymnastic mat hung on the wall.

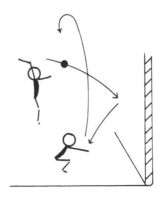

DRILL 288
BLOCK, COVER, 4 PLAYERS, 5 BALLS, NET

One player tosses for a spiker to hit while one player blocks. A fourth player stands behind the blocker and tosses a ball just over the net in front of or to the side of the spiker for the spiker to dig as they land.

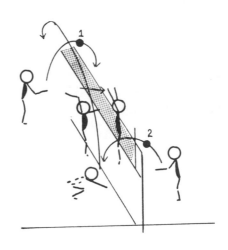

DRILL 289
BLOCK, COVER, 3 PLAYERS, 1 BALL, NET, BLOCKING BOARD

One player tosses a ball up for a player to spike. The tosser then moves in to cover and dig the rebound. A third player holds a blocking board on the other side of the net. The spiker hits at varying speeds into the blocking board.

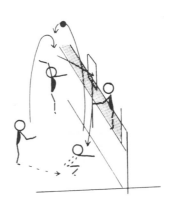

DRILL 290
BLOCK, COVER, 3 PLAYERS, 10 BALLS, NET

One blocker. One player tosses for an attacker to jump and spike deliberately into a block. The attacker must dig the rebound.

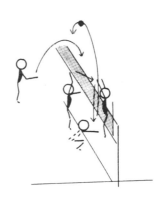

DRILL 291
BLOCK, COVER, 5 PLAYERS, 10 BALLS, NET, BENCH

Two players stand on a bench to block. One player tosses a ball for a player to spike deliberately into the block. The tosser and a fifth player move in to cover and dig the blocked ball. Rotate after 15 hits.

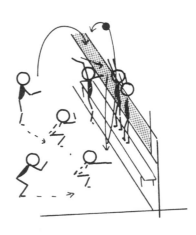

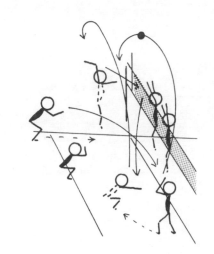

DRILL 292
BLOCK, COVER, SET, SPIKE, BLOCK,
5 PLAYERS, 10 BALLS, NET

Two players block. The spiker tosses a ball to the setter and then deliberately hits into the block. A fifth player covers behind the spiker and the setter covers beside. All three must be ready to dig the rebound. If possible, keep the drill continuous by digging, setting and spiking again.

DRILL 293
BLOCK, COVER, SPIKE, SET, BLOCK,
12 PLAYERS, COACH, 20 BALLS, NET

Three players block and six players play offense on the other side. The coach tosses a ball over the net for the team to pass, set and spike deliberately into the block. The team must cover, dig, set and spike again. As soon as a ball is dead, the coach tosses another ball into play. Rotate positions in groups of three from blocking to back-court to front-court to blocking. A fourth group of three can chase balls and feed them to the coach.

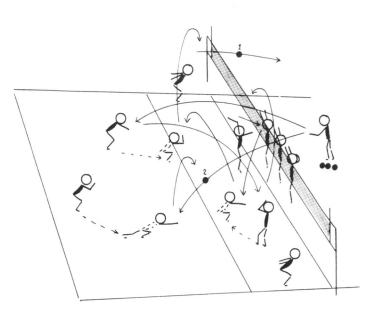

WHEN YOU DECIDE
IT CANNOT BE DONE
STAND BACK AND WATCH
THE OTHER FELLOW DO IT.

OBJECTIVE
To improve setting skills

DRILL 294
SET, 2 PLAYERS, 20 BALLS, NET, TARGET NET, BASKET

The target net is attached to the net at position #4. A tosser throws balls continuously to a setter who starts in the setting place and sets to the target net. Move the target to position #2 and do the same with back sets. Collect the balls and repeat.

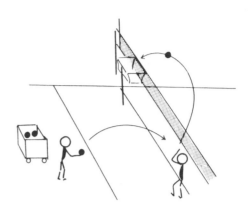

DRILL 295
SET, 3 PLAYERS, 20 BALLS, NET, TARGET NET, BASKET, CHAIR

The target net is attached to the net at position #4. A tosser throws balls to two setters who alternate setting to the target. After setting, the setter must move out and around the chair (on the attack line) and then move in to set. The extra player collects balls and puts them in the basket. Move the target to position #2 and do the same with back sets.

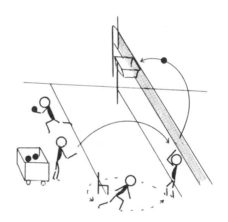

DRILL 296
SET, 5 PLAYERS, 20 BALLS, NET, TARGET NET, BASKET, CHAIR

The target net is attached to the net at position #4. A target player catches balls at position #2. The chair is placed on the attack line. A tosser throws balls up close to the net. Two setters alternate setting, one forward and the other backward. They move out around the chair after each set. The target player catches balls and throws them back to the tosser. The fifth player chases other balls and returns them to the basket. Setters change from forward to backward sets every 20 times.

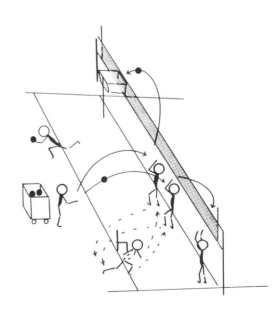

GAME 297
SET, 4 PLAYERS, 20 BALLS,
NET, TARGET NET

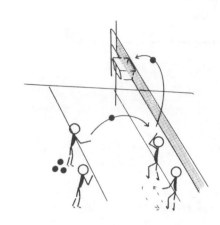

Two players per team. The target net is attached to the net at any position. One partner tosses 15 balls for the partner to set. The other team does the same. Then change places between tossers and setters. Keep score on the total number of balls set into the target net.

GAME 298
SET, 2-4 PLAYERS, 2-4 BALLS,
NET, TARGET NET

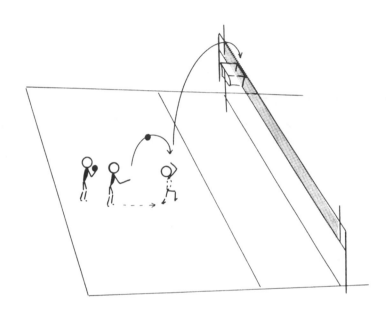

The target net is attached to the net at any position. Each player has a ball. The first player either bounces the ball on the floor or tosses the ball up and moves under the ball and sets to the target. If the ball is set into the target, the next player must repeat the same set from the same place. If the player fails to make the set, they receive one penalty point. If the target is missed, the next player in order may set from any place and with any style. A player is eliminated from the game once they have a total of 5 penalty points. If a player does score with the same set as the previous player, they score a plus and take one penalty point away from their score.

DRILL 299
SET, 3 PLAYERS, 2 BALLS, NET

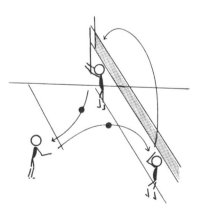

One player tosses to the setter who sets to position #4. The third player catches the ball and throws it back to the tosser. Use two balls and set as rapidly as possible. Do the same with back sets to position #2.

DRILL 300
SET, 4 PLAYERS, 2 BALLS, NET, CHAIR

One player tosses to two setters who alternate setting to a target player who catches the ball and throws it back to the tosser. The target player holds the hands up high and the setters try to have the ball drop right into the target player's hands. The setter must move out around the chair after each set. Use 2 balls and set as rapidly as possible. You could also have the target player stand on a chair.

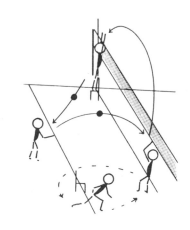

DRILL 301
SET, 5 PLAYERS, 2 BALLS, NET, CHAIR

One player tosses to two setters who alternate setting to target players at positions #4 and #2. The target players catch the balls and throw them back to the tosser. The chair is placed on the attack line and the setters must move out around the chair after each set. Do first with one setter setting only forward while the other only sets backward. Then have each setter alternate forward and backward sets.

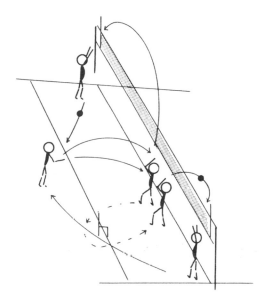

DRILL 302
SET, 5 PLAYERS, 2 BALLS, NET, CHAIR

One player tosses to two setters who alternate setting to position #3. Two players alternate approaching and jumping as if to attack at position #3, but they jump, land and return the ball to the tosser. The objective is to develop consistency with the height of the set and timing with the spiker. Repeat as rapidly as possible and rotate the tosser into the drill.

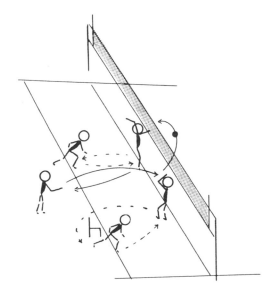

DRILL 303
SET, 5 PLAYERS, 2 BALLS, NET, CHAIR

The chair is placed about 1 metre away from the net in the setting place. A player tosses balls up to the mid-court area. Two setters alternate moving out to set the ball to position #4 and after each set they must move back around the chair and then out to make the next set. Two attackers alternate approaching, jumping and catching the set and then return it to the tosser. If the set is good, the attacker yells "good" to the setter. If it is bad, they yell "bad" or "O.K." for an adequate set. The purpose of this drill is to have the setter learn to set from other than the ideal place. Do the same drill with back sets to position #2. Start with easy tosses until the skill is reasonable and then gradually make it more difficult for the setter. Have the setters move back and sit on the chair until the ball is tossed.

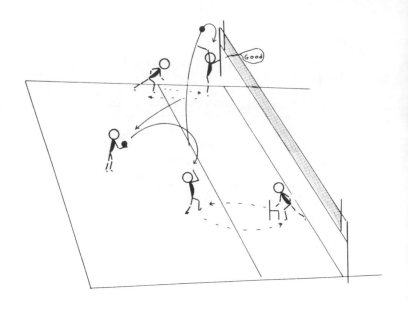

DRILL 304
SET, 3 PLAYERS, 2 BALLS, NET

One player tosses balls to various places close to the net. The setter must move under the ball and set to a target player at position #4 who catches the ball and returns it to the tosser. Use two balls and set as rapidly as possible. Do the same with back sets to position #2 and sets to position #3.

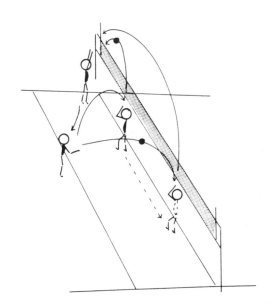

DRILL 305
SET, 5 PLAYERS, 2 BALLS, NET

One player tosses balls to the setting place. Two setters alternate moving under the ball and setting play sets (low, medium, shoot, etc.) to two attackers who alternate approaching, jumping and catching the ball and then returning the ball to the tosser. The attackers should tell the setter if the set was good, bad or adequate each time.

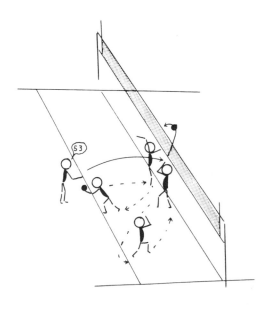

OBJECTIVE
To develop ability to set bad passes

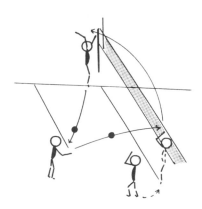

DRILL 306
SET, 3 PLAYERS, 2 BALLS, NET

One player tosses balls flat toward the top of the net. The setter must move in, jump and set to a target player. The target player can approach, jump and catch the set and return it to the tosser. Use two balls and move as rapidly as possible. Practice both front and back sets as well as low sets.

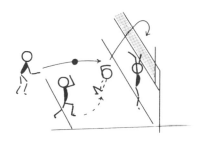

DRILL 307
SET, 3 PLAYERS, 2 BALLS, NET

One player tosses balls low toward the setting place. The setter must squat or "screw under" and set to the target player. The target player catches the ball and throws it back to the tosser. Practice both front and back sets as well as high and low sets.

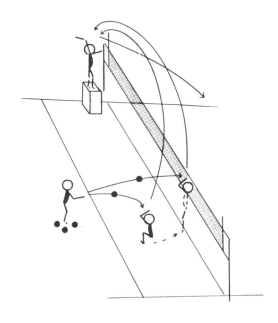

DRILL 308
SET, 3 PLAYERS, 20 BALLS, NET, PLATFORM

One player tosses balls at various trajectories to the setting place. The setter must adjust to each ball and jump, squat or roll and set the ball to an attacker standing on the platform at position #4. The attacker spikes the ball whenever possible and catches those that are less than ideal. Keep count of the total number out of 15 that are spiked.

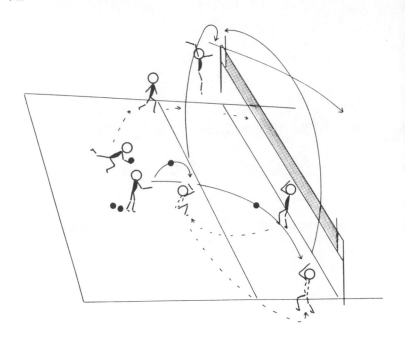

DRILL 309
SET, SPIKE, 5-10 PLAYERS,
20 BALLS, NET

One player tosses balls at varying heights to various places on the court. The setter must move under the ball and set to spikers at one of the attack positions. Make the tosses as difficult as the setter can handle. Set both front and back sets. Spikers return balls to the tosser.

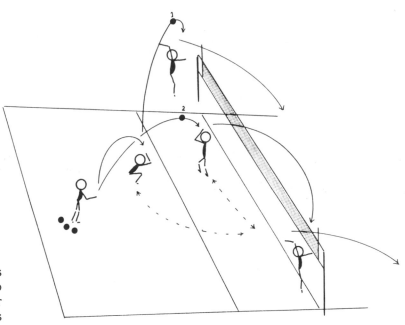

DRILL 310
SET, SPIKE, 6-12 PLAYERS,
20 BALLS, NET

One player tosses at varying heights to various places on the court. Two setters alternate setting, one to position #4 and the other to position #2. One or more players attack at each position. The extra players chase balls and feed them to the tosser. Have the setters change targets after 45 sets.

**WHEN THE WHIP TOUCHES
THE THOROUGHBRED,
HE RESPONDS WITH ALL
HIS COURAGE...WHEN
A MULE FEELS THE WHIP,
HE BALKS AND SULKS.**

DRILL 311
SET, SPIKE, 6-12 PLAYERS,
20 BALLS, NET, PLATFORM, BASKET

The platform is set up on the other side of the net in position #2. The attacker tosses a ball to the setter who sets for the attacker to spike at position #4. The setter moves to cover. As soon as the ball is spiked, a player on the platform drops another ball to the setter to set for the spiker to hit again. The spiker then chases the balls and feeds them to the tossers. The object of this drill is to simulate a blocked ball that must be set immediately by the setter.

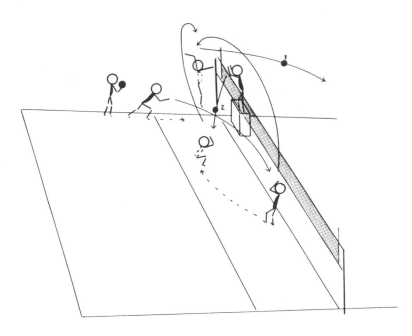

OBJECTIVE
To develop control with the tip

DRILL 312
TIP, 3 PLAYERS, 1 BALL, NET

One player starts the drill by serving or throwing the ball over the net to an attacker who passes to the setter. The ball is set and the attacker tips over the net to the first player who then passes the ball up. The setter ducks under the net and sets for the first player to tip. Continue.

Start by tipping directly to the player on the other side and gradually tip away from the player to make the pass more difficult. See how many times in a row the ball can be tipped without losing control.

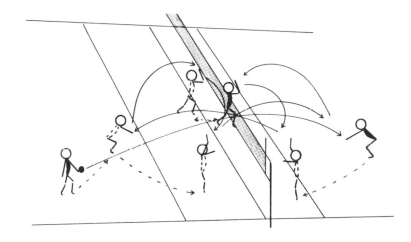

GAME 313
TIP, 4 PLAYERS, 1 BALL, NET

The players pass, set and tip the ball back and forth over the net. Start by using only one quarter of the court, then one-half of the court and then the entire court as the skills develop. Play to 8 points and then change sides and score as in volleyball. Start with easy serves and then more difficult serves as the skill improves.

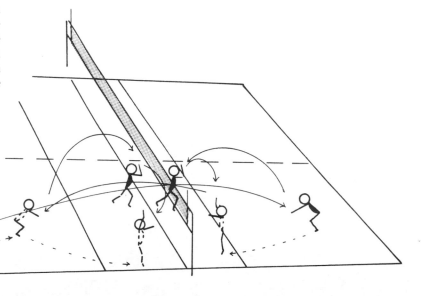

OBJECTIVE
To align the body to the direction of the attack while spiking

DRILL 314
SPIKE, 1 PLAYER, 1 BALL, WALL

The player stands about 5 metres from a wall facing to the left or right. The player tosses the ball up, jumps, rotates and spikes the ball to the floor and wall. Gradually increase the degrees of rotation.

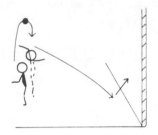

DRILL 315
SPIKE, 2 PLAYERS, 1 BALL

Two players stand about 10 metres apart. The player faces to the left or right, tosses the ball straight up, jumps, rotates and spikes the ball to the floor directly toward their partner. Gradually increase the degrees of rotation.

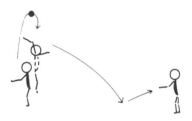

DRILL 316
SPIKE, 2 PLAYERS, 5 BALLS, NET

The spiker stands beside the net facing to the left or right. The other player tosses the ball straight up high for the spiker to jump, rotate and spike. Gradually increases the degrees of rotation. Toss from various directions.

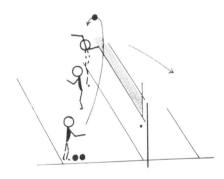

DRILL 317
SPIKE, 5 PLAYERS, 10 BALLS, NET

Two players alternate tossing balls from various directions to a spiker who must recover after each hit, reorient themself to the ball and spike it. The reorientation will be a mixture of feet placement before jumping and body rotation in the air. Aim at a chair as a target.

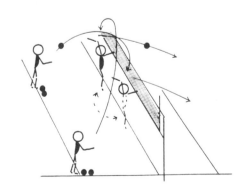

OBJECTIVE
To improve the ability to spike balls that are set from various places and at varying heights

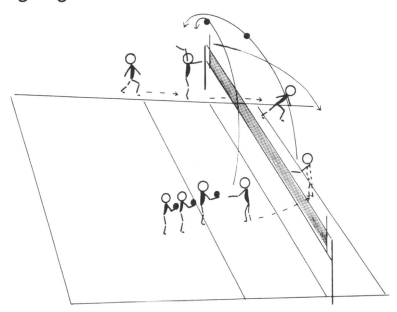

DRILL 318
SPIKE, 10-12 PLAYERS, COACH, 10 BALLS, NET

Two players start in the hitting line without balls. The other players start in the feeding line with balls and hand them to the coach as rapidly as possible and move to the hitting line. After hitting, the spiker chases their ball and goes to the feeding line. The coach starts tossing high balls from the normal setting spot and continues tossing without stopping for 15 to 20 minutes. Toss about 50 balls in a row from one place at the same height and then slowly move to a different place, toss balls at a different height, toss to a different place along the net, or back further from the net. Toss about 50 balls and change again.

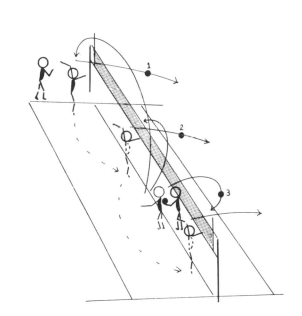

DRILL 319
SPIKE, 6 PLAYERS, COACH, 10 BALLS, NET

The coach tosses 3 balls in a row to a spiker. The first toss is to position #4, the second to position #3, and the third to position #2. The spiker must recover and move rapidly after each hit. A second player does the same followed again by the first spiker. The other players chase balls and feed them to the coach. Change when the two spikers get tired. Vary the height of the toss.

ITS WHAT YOU LEARN
AFTER YOU KNOW IT ALL
THAT COUNTS.

DRILL 320
SPIKE, SET, 6-10 PLAYERS, 10 BALLS, NET

One player tosses balls to a setter who sets three balls in a row to a spiker; the first to position #4, the second to position #3, and the third to position #2. The spiker must recover and move rapidly after each hit. A second spiker does the same, followed again by the first spiker. The other players chase balls and feed them to the tosser. Change the order of the position sequence from #4-3-2 to #2-3-4 or #3-4-2.

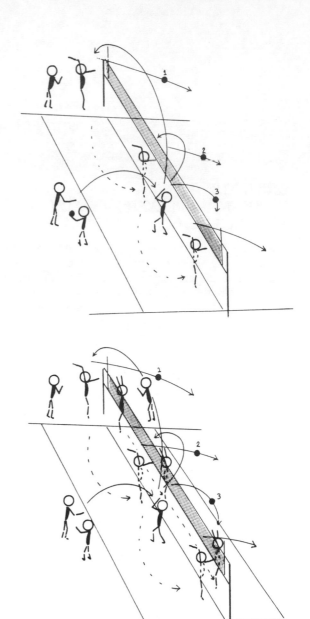

DRILL 321
SPIKE, SET, BLOCK, 10 PLAYERS, 10 BALLS, NET

One player tosses balls to a setter who sets 3 balls in a row to a spiker; the first to position #4, the second to position #3 and the third to position #2. A blocker attempts to block at all three positions. A second spiker and blocker do the same, followed again by the first spiker and blocker. The other players chase balls and feed them to the tosser. Change when the spikers get tired.

DRILL 322
SPIKE, PASS, SET, 5 PLAYERS, 10 BALLS, NET

One player throws or serves balls over the net to the spiker. The spiker passes to the setter and then moves in to spike. The setter calls a play set before the pass and calls a different play set each time. The other players chase balls and feed them to the tosser. Continue until the spiker is tired and then rotate.

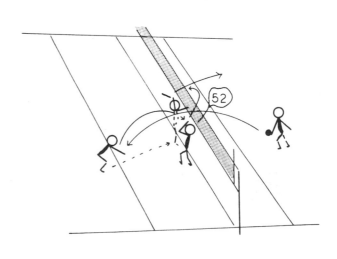

OBJECTIVE
To improve the ability to set and close the block

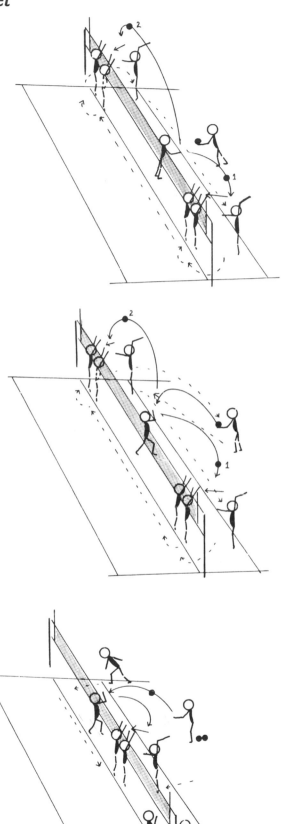

DRILL 323
BLOCK, SPIKE, 6-8 PLAYERS, 10 BALLS, NET

One player alternates tossing to spikers at positions #2 and #4. Three players start as blockers on the other side. Players rotate one position clockwise after they spike or block. The middle blocker will block at position #2, then at position #4, and then on the outside at position #4, and then move to attack at position #2. The spikers attack at position #2, then at position #4 and then block on the other side of the net outside at position #2.

DRILL 324
BLOCK, SET, SPIKE, 8-10 PLAYERS, 10 BALLS, NET

Same as the previous drill except that a setter is added and the tosser throws the ball to the setter. The extra players chase balls and feed them to the tosser, or the tosser is eliminated and a tossing line is added to the drill and the blocker, when finished, chases a ball and moves to the end of the tossing line, and from the front of the tossing line to the first hitting position.

DRILL 325
BLOCK, SET, SPIKE, 8-10 PLAYERS, 10 BALLS, NET

Three blockers, 1 setter, 3 spikers and 1 tosser. One player tosses the ball to the setter who sets in random order to each of the front—row spikers. The blockers shift and establish a two player block each time. Start with high sets to allow blockers time to move. Gradually lower the height of the set. Attackers always hit in a predetermined direction and attempt to hit into the block to begin with. The extra players chase balls and feed them to the tosser.

OBJECTIVE
To improve spiking and blocking skills

DRILL 326
BLOCK, SPIKE, 6-10 PLAYERS, COACH, 10 BALLS, NET

The coach tosses a ball for the first player in the attacking line to hit. Two players block. After hitting, the spiker crosses under the net and replaces the outside blocker as the outside blocker becomes the middle blocker. The middle blocker chases the ball and moves to the end of the hitting line. Continue.

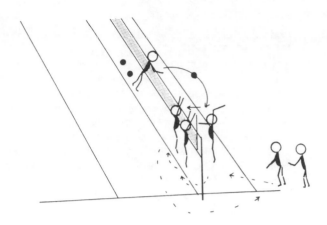

DRILL 327
BLOCK, SPIKE, SET, 6-10 PLAYERS, COACH, 10 BALLS, NET

Add a setter to the previous drill. The coach tosses the ball to the setter. Do this drill from all three positions.

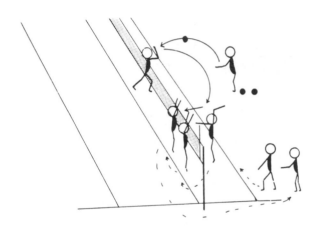

DRILL 328
BLOCK, SPIKE, SET, 6-10 PLAYERS, COACH, 10 BALLS, NET

Add a passer to the previous drill. The coach either tosses or serves the ball over the net. You may either rotate from passer to hitter to outside blocker to middle blocker to passer — keep the setter constant, or you may also rotate the setting position as well — middle blocker to setter to passer to hitter, etc.

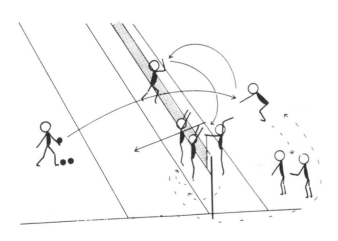

DRILL 329
BLOCK, SPIKE, SET, 6-10 PLAYERS, COACH, 10 BALLS, NET

The coach tosses a ball to a setter who sets to position #4. The first player in the attacking line spikes and two players block. If the block is successful, the attacker replaces the outside blocker, the outside blocker moves to middle blocker and the middle blocker chases the ball and goes to the end of the attacking line. However, if the block is not successful, the attacker chases the ball and goes to the end of the attacking line.

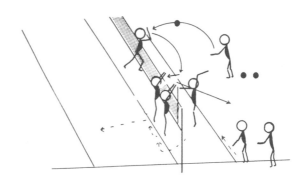

DRILL 330
BLOCK, SPIKE, 6 PLAYERS, COACH, 10 BALLS, NET

Start with three players blocking and three players hitting. The coach tosses the first ball to position #4 for an attacker to spike while the middle and front—row players block. The coach then tosses the next ball to position #2 for the second attacker to hit as the middle and front left players block. Now rotate positions. The first attacker replaces the front right blocker, the front right blocker moves to middle blocker, the middle blocker moves to front left and the front left blocker moves to hit from position #2. The position #2 hitter moves across to hit from position #4. A variation is to hit all 10 balls before rotating positions.

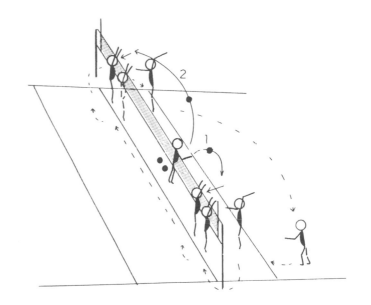

DRILL 331
BLOCK, SPIKE, SET, 7 PLAYERS, COACH, 10 BALLS, NET

Add a setter to the previous drill and have the coach toss the ball to the setter. Then add a passer and the coach tosses or serves the ball over the net to the passer. Rotate from #4 hitter, to right front blocker, to middle blocker, to left front blocker, to #2 hitter, to passer to #4 hitter.

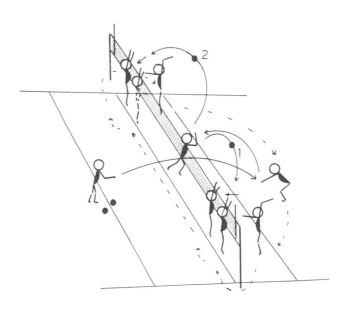

OBJECTIVE
To improve skill execution in order of game sequence

DRILL 332
SPIKE, BLOCK, 3 PLAYERS,
10 BALLS, NET

(A) One player tosses the ball alternately to the players on opposite sides of the net. While one spikes, the other blocks. (B) As soon as the player blocks, they must move back to get ready to hit.

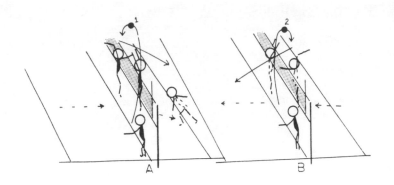

DRILL 333
SPIKE, PASS, SET, 3 PLAYERS,
10 BALLS, NET

One player tosses a ball over the net for the spiker to pass to the setter and then move in to spike. The spiker must recover quickly to pass the next ball. Vary the difficulty of the pass and the height and place of the set. Rotate after 15 balls.

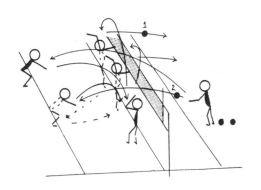

DRILL 334
SPIKE, PASS, SET, 3 PLAYERS,
10 BALLS, NET

(A) One player tosses a ball over the net for the spiker to pass to the setter and then move in to spike. As soon as the setter sets, the tosser throws another ball over the net for (B) the setter to pass and the spiker to set and the setter then spikes. Continue as rapidly as the skill level permits.

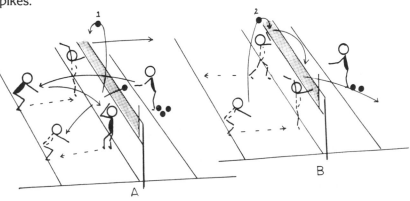

DRILL 335
SPIKE, COVER, SET, 6 PLAYERS,
10 BALLS, NET, BENCH

Two players stand on the bench to block. (A) One player tosses a ball over the net for the spiker to pass to the setter and then move in to spike. The spiker deliberately spikes into the block at half speed (B) and then either the spiker or the setter must recover the rebound. The ball is then set and spiked into court (no block). The sixth player chases balls and feeds them to the tosser.

DRILL 336
SPIKE, BLOCK, PASS, SET,
8 PLAYERS, 20 BALLS, NET

One player on each side of the net to toss. Two front-row players and one back-row player on each side of the net. (A) To start the drill, a ball is tossed over the net for a back-row player to pass to one of the front-row players to set and the other to spike. Two players on the other side block. The spiker deliberately spikes into the block and the other two players must recover the rebound, set and spike again. (B) If the ball is not blocked or if control is lost, a new ball is tossed over the net (alternate sides for the toss). Rotate positions after 15 hits or when a goal is reached.

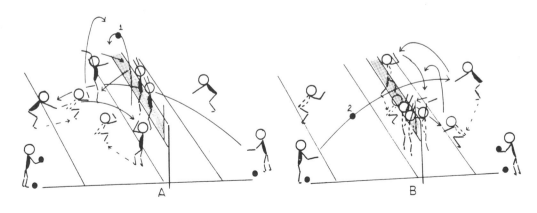

DRILL 337
ALL GAME SKILLS, 12 PLAYERS,
COACH, 20 BALLS, NET

Two teams of six. The coach serves to one team and the two teams play until the ball is dead. The coach quickly serves another ball to start play again. Allow very little time to set up to receive the serve. Rotate front and back row after 15 serves, then rotate and serve to the other team. Serve easy to younger teams and tougher to more skilled teams.

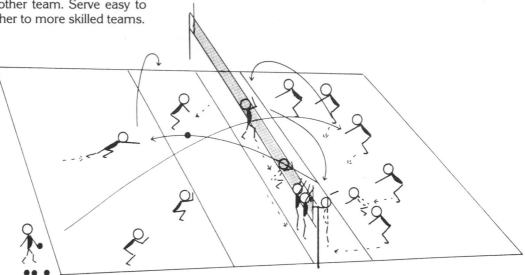

DRILL 338
ALL GAME SKILLS, 12 PLAYERS,
COACH, 20 BALLS, NET

Two teams of six. The coach starts by serving to one team and moves to the side of the court. As soon as the ball is dead, the coach tosses a new ball into play. Repeat. The coach can toss more than one ball, can toss at the player who made the error, or at a player who did not move to cover.

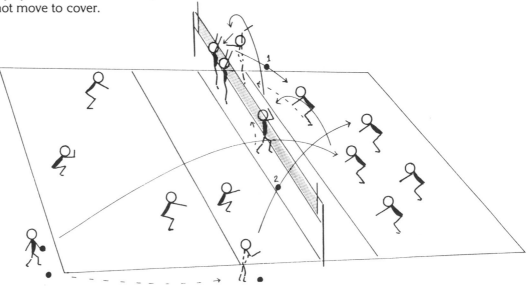

GAME 339
SPIKE, BLOCK, SET, 5 PLAYERS,
10 BALLS, NET

A tosser throws a ball to the setter who sets and the spiker deliberately hits the first ball into the block. Two players block. The tosser quickly tosses a second ball for the spiker to hit (no approach), but this time the spiker tries to avoid the block and score. Score +3 if the second spike is good and -1 if the ball is blocked or hit out. Repeat 10 to 15 hits each and rotate.

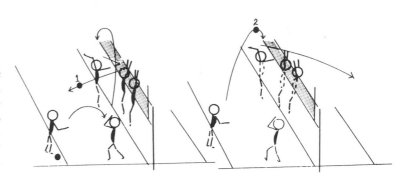

GAME 340
ALL GAME SKILLS, 15 PLAYERS,
20 BALLS, NET

Two teams of six. Two tossers on the sidelines, one on each side of the net. One tosser starts by throwing a ball over the net for a team to pass, set and spike. The other team attempts to block or keep the ball in play. As soon as the ball is dead, the other tosser throws a ball into play. Score points for winning the rally (no side-out). The tossers keep track of the score for the team on their side. Rotate back and front row and tossers after each game. The game can be played with fewer than 6 per team.

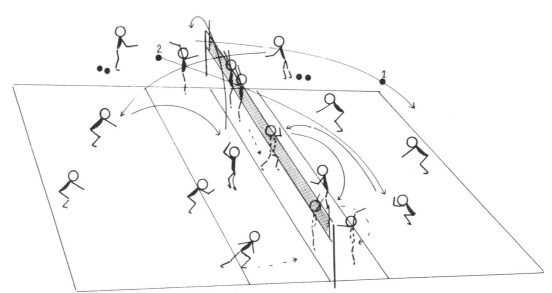

OBJECTIVE
Concentration improvement

DRILL 341
SERVE, 10-12 PLAYERS,
10-12 BALLS, NET

Players serve back and forth over the net toward a target. They must take turns serving and only one at a time shall serve, but with minimal delay. The group must serve 45 serves without a mistake, or hit the larger target every time without missing. Each time a player misses, the groups must start back at zero. The idea is to put pressure on a player once the success count approaches the goal.

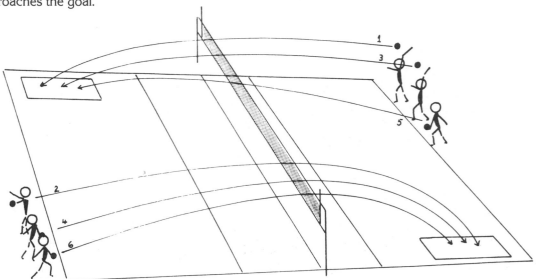

DRILL 342
PASS, 2 PLAYERS, 1 BALL

Two players stand 3 metres apart. One ball is passed back and forth using either the forearm pass or the overhand pass. As soon as a player passes the ball they hold up one, two or three fingers on one hand. The other player must look and identify the number of fingers being held up before passing the ball. For advanced players, delay holding up the fingers.

DRILL 343
PASS, 2 PLAYERS, 2 BALLS

Two players stand 3 metres apart. One ball is passed back and forth using either the forearm pass or the overhand pass. At the same time, a second ball is gently kicked back and forth. Keep both balls going without stopping.

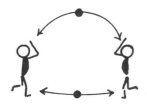

DRILL 344
DIG, 5-10 PLAYERS, 20 BALLS,
NET, 3 PLATFORMS

Three players stand on the platforms and spike or tip in random order at one player on the other side who digs to a target player. The object is to get to a positive score of 10. Score + 1 for the first good pass to target, + 2 for the second, + 3 for the third, + 4 for the fourth, etc. At the same time, a deduction equal to the last positive score is made for each bad pass. Do not accumulate negative totals. Vary the difficulty of the spikes according to the ability level of the players.

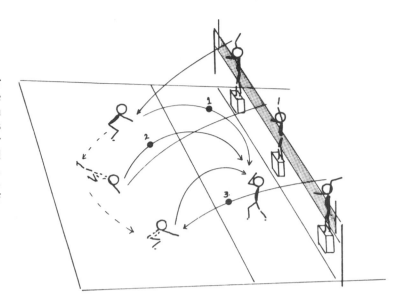

DRILL 345
SPIKE, SET, 8-12 PLAYERS,
COACH, 8-12 BALLS, NET

The coach tosses balls to a setter who alternates setting forward and backward to two lines of spikers. The goal is to spike 45 balls in a row into court. Each time there is a miss, the group starts back at zero. The object is to put pressure on the players as they approach the goal. A variation is to have the coach toss balls over the net to the front player in one line who passes for the setter to set to the front player in the other line. This makes the drill more difficult.

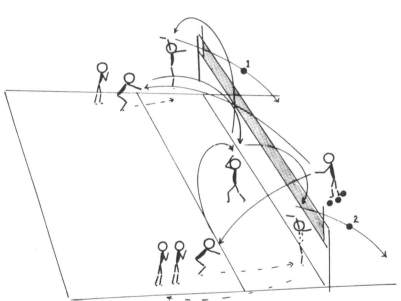

THE TEAM THAT MAKES
THE FEWEST MISTAKES
USUALLY WINS.

DRILL 346
PASS, SET, SPIKE, SERVE,
8-12 PLAYERS, COACH,
10 BALLS, NET

Players work in pairs. The coach and one player from each end serve. One pair starts on reception and must pass, set and spike the ball into court. The next pair do the same. The group must complete 15 successful series without an error. Each time they make a mistake they start at zero. The object is to put pressure on the players as they approach the goal.

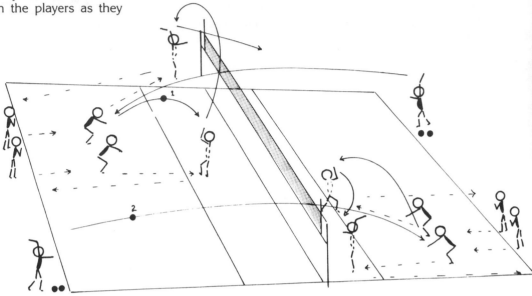

OBJECTIVE
Conditioning and skill improvement

DRILL 347
PASS, SET, SPIKE, BLOCK,
6-10 PLAYERS, 10 BALLS, NET

Three players block. One player tosses balls over the net for the spiker to pass to a setter who sets. The spiker must not be blocked and is not allowed to tip. The spiker must score 5 times in a row before the players rotate. A wipe off is legitimate.

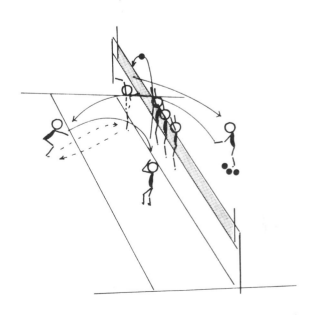

DRILL 348
DIVE, 2-4 PLAYERS, COACH,
20 BALLS

The coach stands at the net and tosses balls in random directions for a player to dive and dig. Continue until the player is exhausted. The extra player chase the balls and feed them to the coach.

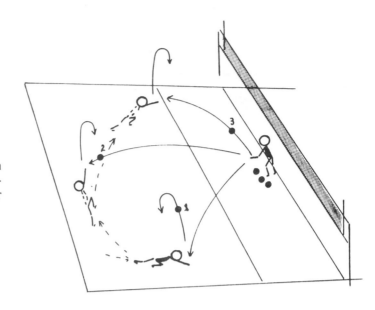

DRILL 349
DIG, 3-6 PLAYERS, COACH,
20 BALLS, CHAIR

The chair is placed on the middle of the back line. The coach stands at the net and tips or spikes balls for the player to dig. The player must first dig from the right side of the court, move back around the chair and dig on the left side of the court. Start with easy tips or spikes for beginners and progress to hard hits or low tips or tosses for advanced players who will have to move to dig the ball in front of the attack line each time.

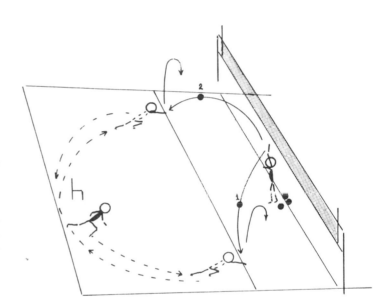

DRILL 350
SPIKE, 2-4 PLAYERS, COACH,
20 BALLS, NET, BASKET

The coach tosses balls for a player to spike continuously. The other players collect balls and keep the basket full. The player quits when the basket is empty or when exhaustion forces the player to quit.

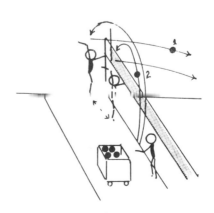

DRILL 351
SPIKE, 6-12 PLAYERS, COACH,
20 BALLS, NET, BASKET, 6 CHAIRS

The balls are in the basket near the coach. Six chairs are lined up in a row beside or at the back of the court spread apart to allow the players to jump over each chair in succession. The coach tosses balls up for the players to spike in turn. After spiking, the player chases the ball and puts it in the basket and then jumps the six chairs in a row before returning to the spiking line.

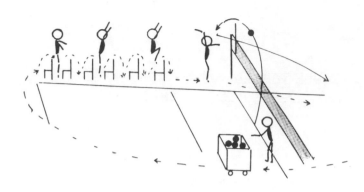

DRILL 352
DIVE, SPIKE, 2-4 PLAYERS,
COACH, 20 BALLS, NET

The coach stands at the net and tosses the first ball for the player to dive and dig, and the second ball for the player to jump and spike. Continue alternating until the player is exhausted or until 30 to 50 balls have been played, or until 15 balls have been spiked successfully into court.

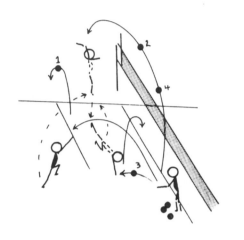

DRILL 353
SET, DIG, SPIKE, 6-10 PLAYERS,
20 BALLS, NET, 2 PLATFORMS

Two players start on platforms on the other side of the net at each sideline and toss, spike and toss sets for a player on the other side. The player must run from side to side along the attack line and first set 10 to 15 balls back to the other side. Then the player must run and dig 10 to 15 balls, and finally run and spike 10 to 15 balls. The extra players chase and feed balls to the platform players. The drill can be done with 2 players running simultaneously if there are enough chasers or can be run without a platform if the spikers attack from in front of the net.

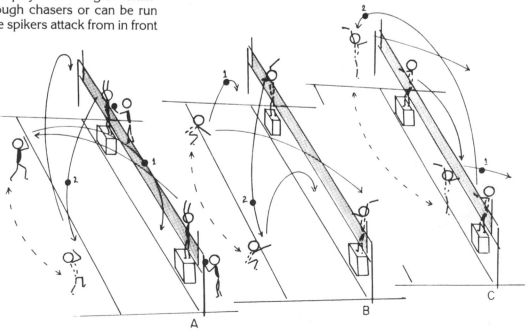

DRILL 354
BLOCK, ATTACK, DIVE, 3-6 PLAYERS, COACH, 20 BALLS, NET

The coach lob spikes a ball for a player to block. The coach then tosses a ball up over the net for the player to spike. The coach then tosses a third ball over the net to the back-court area for the player to dive and dig. Repeat 10 to 15 times or until the player scores 15 — one point for each good block, spike or dig.

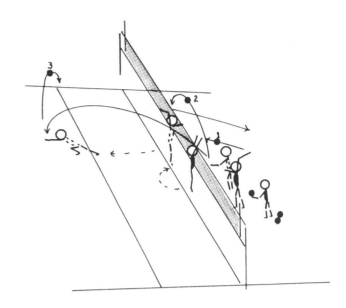

DRILL 355
DIG, SET, SPIKE, 3-4 PLAYERS, COACH, PLATFORM, 20 BALLS, NET

The coach spikes or tips balls from the platform at two players who must cover the entire court and dig, set and spike the ball. As soon as the ball is spiked the coach will spike or tip a new ball. Repeat as rapidly as skill level permits and extend the players to their limits. The extra players chase balls and feed them to the coach.

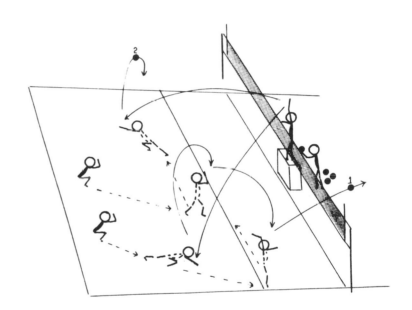

THE NEXT EFFORT
IS
THE IMPORTANT ONE.

DRILL 356
DIG, SET, SPIKE, 4-8 PLAYERS,
20 BALLS, NET

One tosser on each side of the net. Two players start on one back line and do one or two pushups or situps. They then race across under the net to the other court where a player tosses a ball up for the two players to dig, set and spike. The two players then repeat the same in the other direction and continue until exhausted.

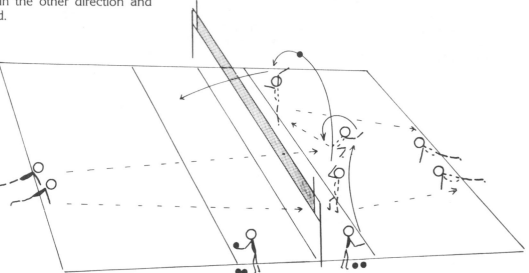

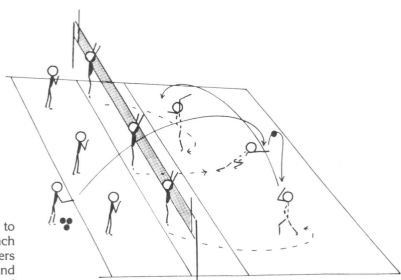

DRILL 357
PASS, SET, SPIKE, 6-9 PLAYERS,
COACH, 20 BALLS, NET

Groups of three. The first three players jump to block on the command of the coach. The coach then tosses a ball over the net and the three players must race under the net, dig the ball up, set and spike and return to repeat as soon as the second group has finished the same. Repeat with the two groups alternating as fast as possible. This drill can be run in pairs as well.

PART V

TRANSITION DRILLS

OBJECTIVE
To teach transition from offense to defense (serve to dig)

DRILL 358
TRANSITION, SERVE TO DIG,
4 PLAYERS, 10 BALLS, NET

One player serves and then moves in to dig. The spiker on the other side passes to a setter and then spikes or tips directly at the server who digs towards a partner near the net. The partner then runs back to serve and the drill continues.

OBJECTIVE
To teach transition from offense to defense (cover to attack)

DRILL 359
TRANSITION, COVER TO ATTACK,
8 PLAYERS, 20 BALLS, NET

Two front-row players, one back-row player and one tosser on each side of the net. (A) One tosser throws a ball over the net for a back-row player to pass and then move in to cover. Their team-mates set and spike deliberately into the block. Try to cover and keep the ball in play. If the ball is not blocked, the same tosser immediately throws another ball over the net for the attackers to pass, set and spike again. (B) Once this second ball is dead, the other tosser repeats the same sequence from the other side.

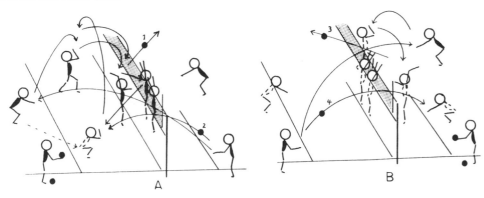

133

OBJECTIVE
To teach transition from offense to defense (attack to block)

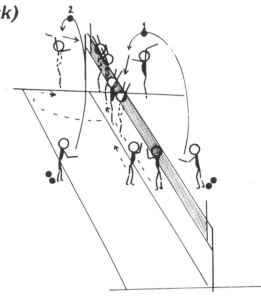

DRILL 360
TRANSITION, SPIKE TO BLOCK, 6 PLAYERS, 20 BALLS, NET

One tosser, one spiker, one middle blocker on each side of the net. A tosser on one side tosses a ball up for the spiker to hit. The spiker and middle blocker on the other side block. The tosser on the other side then tosses a ball for the spiker on that side to hit. Continue. Extra players chase balls and feed them to the tossers.

DRILL 361
TRANSITION, SPIKE TO BLOCK, 6 PLAYERS, 20 BALLS, NET

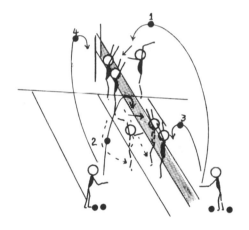

One tosser, one outside attacker, one middle attacker on each side of the net. The tossers alternate tossing on each side of the net and also alternate tossing first to the outside attacker and then to the middle attacker. The players on the other side block, first outside and the next time middle. Continue. Do as rapidly as the skill level permits. Extra players chase balls and feed them to the tossers.

DRILL 362
TRANSITION, SPIKE TO BLOCK, 8 PLAYERS, 20 BALLS, NET

One tosser, one setter, one outside attacker, one middle attacker on each side of the net. (A) The tossers alternate tossing on each side of the net to the setter who alternates setting first to the outside attacker and then to the middle attacker. The players on the other side block. (B) The tosser can throw the ball just as the spiker on the other side contacts the ball to force a very quick transition. The setter can set low sets to speed up the transition. Extra players chase balls and feed them to the tossers.

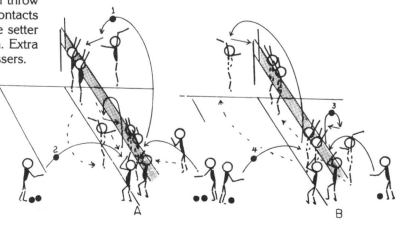

DRILL 363
TRANSITION, SPIKE TO BLOCK,
8 PLAYERS, 20 BALLS, NET

The drill is the same as in the previous drill except that the setter now sets in random order to either of the attackers. The setter could also set to any place along the net forcing the players to shift much further to block or spike.

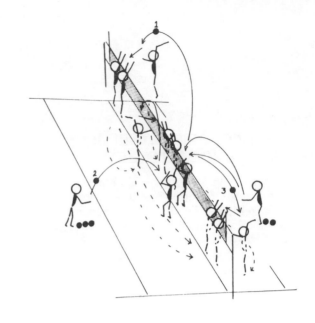

DRILL 364
TRANSITION, SPIKE TO BLOCK,
8 PLAYERS, 20 BALLS, NET

Three front-row players, one tosser on each side of the net. The tossers alternate tossing on each side of the net for an attacker to spike while the players on the other side block. Put up a two or three player block. The tosser must throw as quickly as the skill level will allow to force a quick transition. The tosser should not toss to the same position as the previous tosser, but should force the blockers to shift. That is, shift from a middle attack to an outside hit, or from an attack at position #2 to a block at position #4. Start with high tosses and then gradually lower the height to force a faster transition.

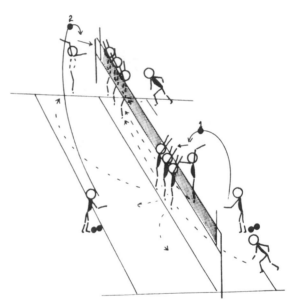

KEEP ON YOUR TOES
AND YOU'LL NEVER BE
CAUGHT FLAT FOOTED.

OBJECTIVE
To teach transition from offense
to defense (cover to dig)

DRILL 365
TRANSITION: COVER TO DIG,
2 PLAYERS, 1 BALL, NET, PLATFORM

One partner stands on the platform on the other side of the net and tosses a ball down simulating a blocked ball forcing the player to dig the ball up high to the tosser. The player then moves backward to a specific back—row position. The tosser now spikes a ball at the player to be dug back up high. The player runs under the ball, catches it and hands it to the tosser. Repeat as quickly as the skill level will allow. Do for all back-row positions.

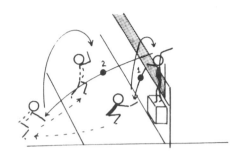

DRILL 366
TRANSITION: COVER TO DIG,
3 PLAYERS, 2 BALLS, NET, PLATFORM

The same as the previous drill except that a setter is added to catch each ball that is passed. Use two balls and the setter immediately throws the ball to the player on the platform so that the drill can be run rapidly.

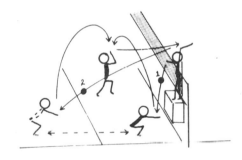

DRILL 367
TRANSITION: COVER TO DIG,
3 PLAYERS, 2 BALLS, NET

A spiker jumps and tosses a ball down on a player simulating a blocked ball. The digger, who has moved in to cover, passes the ball up high to a setter. Meanwhile the setter has thrown a second ball to the spiker. The digger moves back to one of the designated back-court positions. The spiker tosses the second ball up, jumps and spikes it at the digger who passes to the setter. Repeat as rapidly as skill level permits. Do for all three back-court positions.

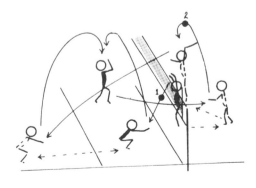

DRILL 368
TRANSITION: COVER TO DIG,
9-12 PLAYERS, 10 BALLS, NET

A team of six players on one side. Three front-row players on the other side, each with a ball. One of the players on the team is a tosser and tosses in random order to any of the front-row players to move in and spike. All other players move to cover the spiker. The player on the other side of the net opposite the spiker jumps and throws a ball down simulating a blocked ball. The players on the team must cover and pass the blocked ball up to the tosser. Repeat as rapidly as possible. Extra players chase balls. The same drill can be done with the tosser now setting the passed ball to keep the drill continuous.

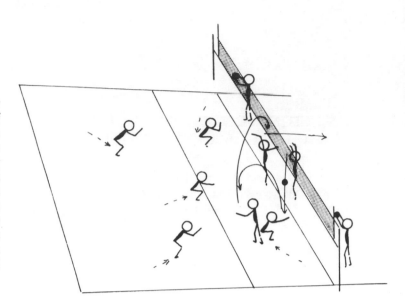

DRILL 369
TRANSITION: COVER TO DIG,
9-12 PLAYERS, 10 BALLS, NET,
3 BLOCKING BOARDS

The same as the previous drill except that three players hold up the blocking boards and the spiker deliberately hits into the board.

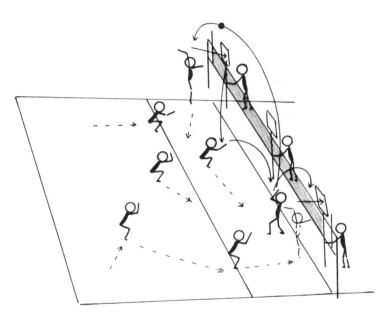

"WIN"
IS SPELLED
H·U·S·T·L·E.

OBJECTIVE
To teach transition from offense to defense (attack to dig)

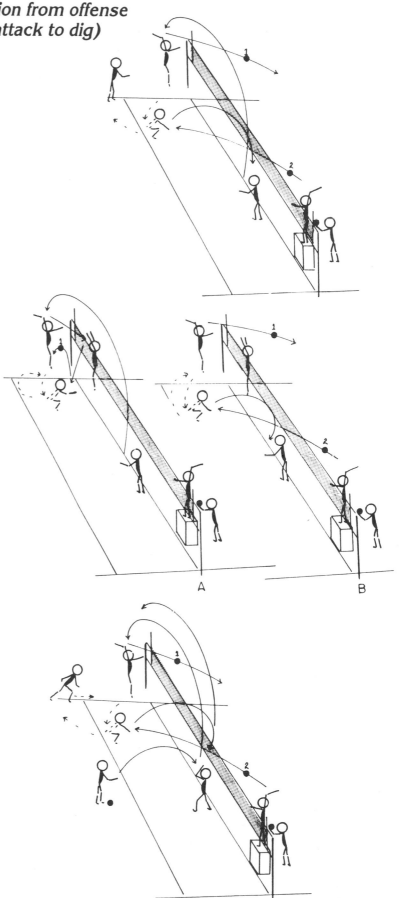

DRILL 370
TRANSITION, ATTACK TO DIG, 3 PLAYERS, COACH, 20 BALLS, NET

The coach stands on the platform on the other side of the net. One player tosses a ball for a player to attack. As soon as the spiker lands, the coach spikes a ball for the attacker to dig up to the tosser. Repeat with the next player in line. Extra players chase balls and feed them to the coach and tosser.

DRILL 371
TRANSITION, ATTACK TO DIG, 4-5 PLAYERS, COACH, 20 BALLS, NET, PLATFORM

The coach stands on the platform on the other side of the net. (A) One player tosses a ball for a player to spike. One or two players block. If the ball is blocked, the spiker attempts to recover the blocked ball. (B) If not, the coach spikes a ball at the spiker to be passed to the tosser. Repeat three times and the next player in line starts. The spiker rotates to blocking. Extra players chase balls and feed them to the coach and tosser.

A   B

DRILL 372
TRANSITION, ATTACK TO DIG, 5 PLAYERS, COACH, 20 BALLS, NET, PLATFORM

The coach stands on the platform on the other side of the net. One player tosses a ball for a setter to set and an attacker to spike. The coach then spikes a ball at the attacker to dig to the setter. If the ball is successfully dug to the setter, the ball is set to the next attacker in line and the drill continues. If not, the tosser throws a new ball to the setter. The extra players chase balls and feed them to the coach and tosser.

DRILL 373
TRANSITION, ATTACK TO DIG,
5-6 PLAYERS, COACH, 20 BALLS,
NET, PLATFORM

The coach stands on the platform on the other side of the net. (A) One player tosses a ball for a setter to set and an attacker to spike. One or two players block. If the ball is blocked, the spiker passes the rebound to the setter who sets for the next attacker in line and the drill continues. (B) If the ball is not blocked or recovered, the coach spikes or tips a ball for the spiker to pass to the setter who sets for the next attacker and the drill continues. Extra players chase balls and feed them to the coach and tosser. Practice from all front-row positions.

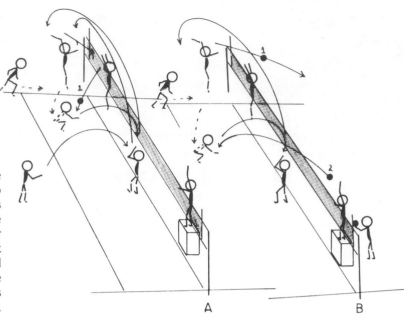

DRILL 374
TRANSITION: ATTACK TO DIG,
6 PLAYERS, COACH, 20 BALLS,
NET, PLATFORM

The coach stands on a platform on the other side of the net. Two players alternate spiking. (A) One player tosses a ball to a setter who sets for an attacker to spike. Two players block. If the ball is blocked, the attacker attempts to dig the ball up for the setter to set to the other attacker. (B) If the ball is not blocked or recovered, the coach spikes or tips a ball for the spiker to pass to the setter who sets for the other attacker and the drill continues. The previous attacker stays to cover, along with the new spiker, and pass to the setter.

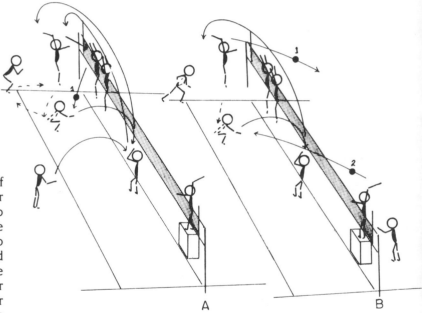

THINK TEAM!

OBJECTIVE
To teach transition from defense to offense (block to dig)

DRILL 375
TRANSITION, BLOCK TO DIG,
2 PLAYERS, COACH, 10 BALLS,
NET, PLATFORM

The coach stands on the platform on the other side of the net. Two players jump to block. As the players come down, the coach tips a ball behind or to the side of the blockers for one of them to dig, the other to set and the digger to spike. Repeat as quickly as the skill level permits. Extra players chase balls and feed them to the coach.

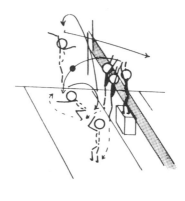

DRILL 376
TRANSITION, BLOCK TO DIG,
4 PLAYERS, 10 BALLS, NET

One player tosses a ball for an attacker to tip. Two players block. The ball is tipped just over the block behind the blockers who land, turn and dig the ball up for the partner to set and the digger to spike. Extra players chase balls and feed them to the tosser.

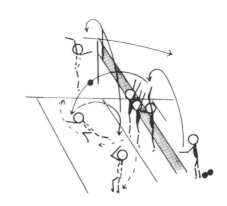

DRILL 377
TRANSITION, BLOCK TO DIG,
5 PLAYERS, 10 BALLS, NET

One player tosses a ball for an attacker to tip. Two players block and another player sets. The ball is tipped just over the block behind the blockers who land, turn and dig the ball up to the setter. The ball is then set to either of the blockers to spike. Repeat again quickly.

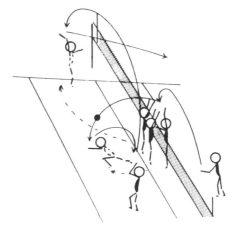

DRILL 378
TRANSITION, BLOCK TO DIG,
2 PLAYERS, 1 BALL, NET

(A) A player tosses a ball for the partner to move in and tip. The tosser crosses under the net and jumps to block. The ball is tipped just over the block. (B) The blocker comes down, turns and digs the tip up high. The tipper crosses under the net as a target setter and catches the ball. Change positions and repeat.

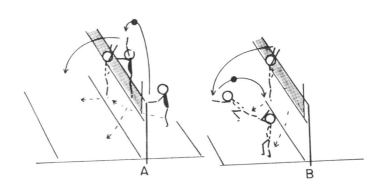

A   B

DRILL 379
TRANSITION, BLOCK TO DIG,
2 PLAYERS, 1 BALL, NET

This is the same as the previous drill except that the target setter now sets the ball, crosses under the net to block and the drill becomes continuous. Toss the ball to start again once control is lost. See how many times the ball can be played over the net continuously.

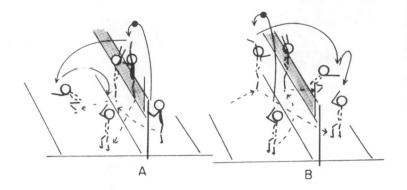

OBJECTIVE
To teach transition from defense
to offense (block to set)

DRILL 380
TRANSITION: BLOCK TO SET,
2 PLAYERS, 1 BALL, NET, PLATFORM

One player stands on the platform and holds a ball up above the net. The setter jumps to block the ball. As the setter lands, the partner tosses a ball for the setter to move under and set high. The setter chases under the set, catches it and gives it to the partner. Repeat.

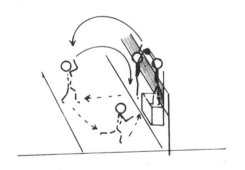

DRILL 381
TRANSITION: BLOCK TO SET,
3 PLAYERS, 20 BALLS, NET,
PLATFORM, BASKET

The balls are in a basket beside the platform. One player stands on the platform and holds a ball up above the net. The setter jumps to block the ball. As the setter lands, the platform player tosses a ball for the setter to set to a third player who spikes. The setter hands a new ball to the platform player. Repeat as rapidly as possible. Spike from all three front-row positions and use a variety of sets depending upon the ability of the setter.

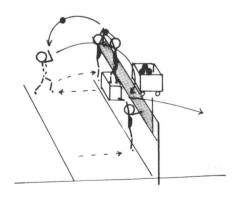

DRILL 382
TRANSITION: BLOCK TO SET,
3 PLAYERS, 20 BALLS, NET, BASKET

One player on the other side tosses a ball up and spikes. The setter blocks. As the setter lands a third player tosses a ball up for the setter to move under and set for that player to attack. Repeat as rapidly as possible. Set to all front-row positions.

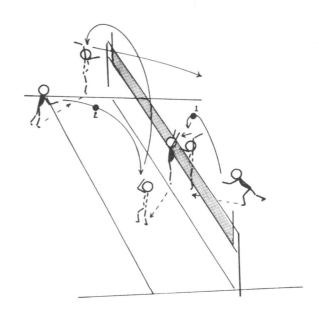

OBJECTIVE
To teach transition from defense
to offense (block to attack)

DRILL 383
TRANSITION: BLOCK TO ATTACK,
2 PLAYERS, COACH, 10 BALLS,
NET, PLATFORM

One player stands on the platform and holds a ball above the net for the player to jump and block. After blocking, the player moves back to make an approach to spike. The coach tosses a ball for the player to spike. Repeat as quickly as skill level permits. Extra players chase balls.

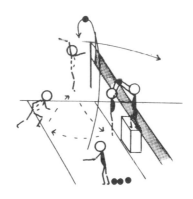

DRILL 384
TRANSITION: BLOCK TO ATTACK,
2 PLAYERS, COACH, 10 BALLS,
NET, PLATFORM

Same as the previous drill except that the player on the platform now spikes the ball for the player to block. Extra players chase balls.

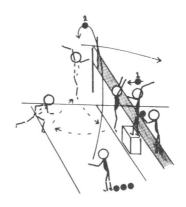

DRILL 385
TRANSITION: BLOCK TO ATTACK, 3 PLAYERS, COACH, 10 BALLS, NET, PLATFORM

One player stands on a platform and spikes balls for a player to block. The coach then tosses a ball to a setter to set for the blocker to spike. The blocker must drop back off the net and then approach to spike. Start with high sets and gradually lower the sets to force a quicker transition.

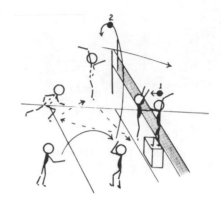

DRILL 386
TRANSITION: BLOCK TO ATTACK, 4 PLAYERS, COACH, 10 BALLS, NET

A player tosses a ball for a player to spike. One player blocks. The coach then tosses a ball to a setter who sets for the blocker to spike. Repeat as rapidly as possible.

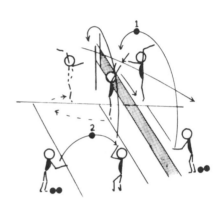

DRILL 387
TRANSITION: BLOCK TO ATTACK, 6 PLAYERS, 20 BALLS, NET

One tosser, one setter, one attacker on each side of the net. (A) The tosser throws a ball to the setter who sets for the attacker. The attacker on the other side blocks. (B) The other tosser immediately tosses a ball for the other setter to set and the blocker to spike. Repeat as rapidly as possible. Extra players chase balls.

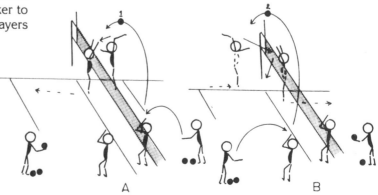

DRILL 388
TRANSITION: BLOCK TO ATTACK, 6 PLAYERS, 20 BALLS, NET

The same as the previous drill except that both the setter and the attacker block forming a two-player block.

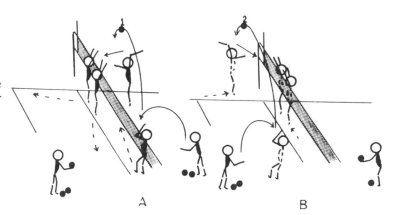

A   B

DRILL 389
TRANSITION: BLOCK TO ATTACK, 3 PLAYERS, COACH, 10 BALLS, NET, PLATFORM

The coach or a player hits from a spiking platform. Two players block. Once the players block they drop back from the net and the coach tosses a second ball to either of the two players. That player then passes to their partner who then sets for the first player to spike. Repeat. A third player feeds balls to the coach.

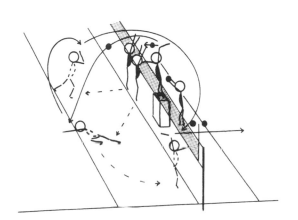

DRILL 390
TRANSITION: BLOCK TO ATTACK, 4 PLAYERS, 10 BALLS, NET

Player 'A' tosses a ball for an attacker to spike. Two players block. If the ball is deflected back to the blockers' side, the blockers drop back from the net and player 'A' tosses a ball for one of the blockers to pass. The other blocker sets for their partner to spike. However, if the ball was blocked back towards the attacker in the first instance, player 'A' tosses the second ball to the attacker to hit again. Repeat. Start by tossing the ball so that the blockers can make an easy pass, and gradually make the toss more difficult.

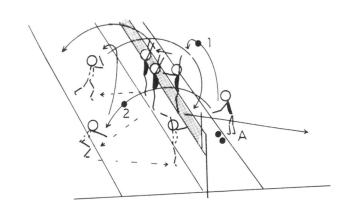

NO ONE
HAS EVER DROWNED
IN SWEAT.

DRILL 391
TRANSITION, BLOCK TO ATTACK,
8-10 PLAYERS, 20 BALLS, NET

One tosser, one setter, one attacker, 1 or 2 back-court players on each side of the net. (A) The ball is tossed to a setter to set for the attacker to spike, while the attacker and setter on the other side block. The back-court players cover and the ball is kept in play. (B) Once a ball is dead, the tosser on the side that blocked last, tosses a new ball to the setter and the drill continues. Extra players chase balls.

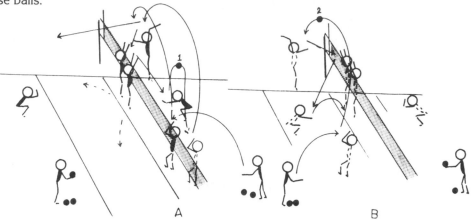

DRILL 392
TRANSITION: BLOCK TO ATTACK,
6 PLAYERS, COACH, 20 BALLS, NET

Three players on each side of the net. The coach starts by serving or tossing a ball over the net for one player to pass, another to set and a third to spike directly at a digger on the same side as the coach. The two players on the same side as the digger and coach attempt to block. The ball is dug to one of the blockers to set for the other to spike and play continues until the ball is dead. If the first spike is not dug or passed, the coach tosses a second ball to be set and spiked to complete the transition from block to attack. Repeat as quickly as skill level permits. Extra players chase balls.

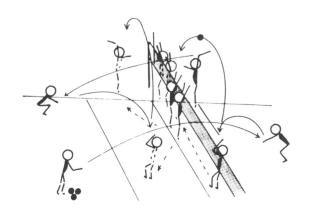

**THE WILL TO WIN
IS NOT NEARLY AS IMPORTANT
AS THE WILL
TO PREPARE TO WIN.**

DRILL 393
TRANSITION: BLOCK TO ATTACK,
6 PLAYERS, 20 BALLS, NET

Player 'A' tosses a ball to a setter who sets for an attacker to spike. Two players block. If the ball is deflected back to the blockers' side, the blockers drop back from the net and player 'B' tosses a ball high for one of the blockers to pass to their partner. The partner sets and the passer spikes. The two players on the other side now block and the drill continues. However, if the ball is blocked back on the attacker's side, the thrower on that side tosses a new ball to be set. Rotate the two tossers into the drill.

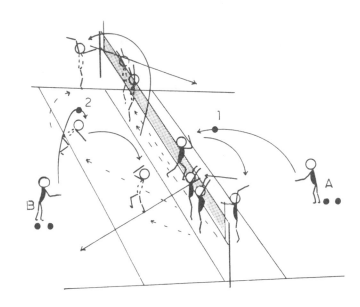

DRILL 394
TRANSITION: BLOCK TO ATTACK,
6 PLAYERS, 20 BALLS, NET

Player 'A' tosses a ball to a setter who sets for an attacker to spike. Two players block. If the ball is deflected back to the blockers' side, the blockers drop back from the net and player 'B' tosses a ball high for one of the blockers to pass to their partner. The partner sets and the passer spikes. The two players on the other side now block and the drill continues. However, if the ball is blocked back on the attacker's side, the thrower on that side tosses a new ball to be set. Rotate the two tossers into the drill.

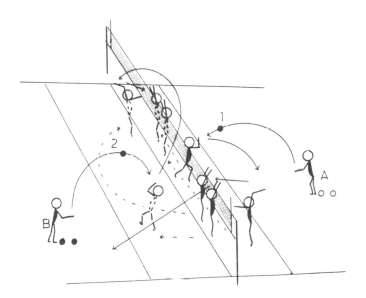

AN UNDEFEATED SEASON
IS WON
ONE GAME AT A TIME.

OBJECTIVE
To teach transition from defense to offense (dig to attack)

DRILL 395
TRANSITION: DIG TO ATTACK, 4-6 PLAYERS, COACH, 10 BALLS, NET, PLATFORM

(A) The coach stands on the platform and spikes cross-court to a player in position #2 or #4. The player digs or passes the ball to the setter, who sets for the player to spike. If the dig is not set, (B) the coach tosses a second ball for the player to spike. One player feeds balls to the coach. Extra players chase balls.

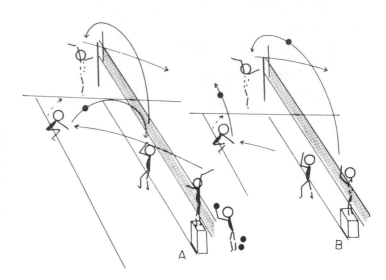

DRILL 396
TRANSITION: DIG TO ATTACK, 6-10 PLAYERS, COACH, 10 BALLS, NET, PLATFORM

(A) The coach stands on the platform and spikes cross-court to a player in position #2 or #4. The player digs or passes the ball to the setter, who sets for the player to spike. Two players block. If the ball is blocked, the attacker passes the blocked ball to the setter, the ball is set and spiked again and continue. (B) If the first pass is not set, the coach tosses a second ball for the player to spike. One player feeds balls to the coach. Extra players chase balls.

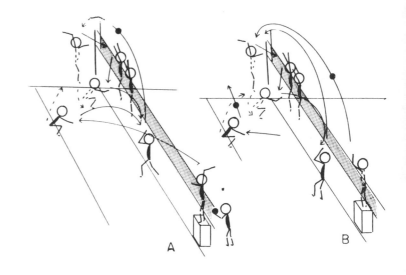

IF YOU THINK YOU ARE INDISPENSABLE, PUT YOUR FINGER IN A BOWL OF WATER, REMOVE FINGER AND LOOK AT HOLE THAT REMAINS.

DRILL 397
TRANSITION: DIG TO ATTACK,
6-10 PLAYERS, COACH, 10 BALLS,
NET, PLATFORM

(A) The coach stands on the platform and spikes either line or cross-court to a back-court player who digs the ball up to the setter. The ball is set for a back-row attack and the player jumps to spike the ball. Two players alternate digging and hitting. (B) If the ball is not set, the coach tosses a second ball for the player to spike. One player feeds balls to the coach. Extra players chase balls.

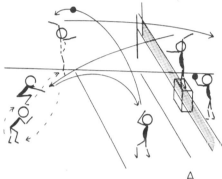
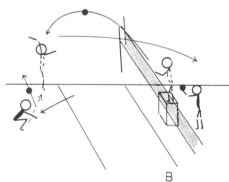

A   B

DRILL 398
TRANSITION: DIG TO ATTACK,
6 PLAYERS, COACH, 20 BALLS, NET,
PLATFORM

A team of six on one side of the net. The coach spikes or tips a ball from the platform and the team dig, set and spike. The coach then spikes a second ball and this time the team blocks and plays defense. The coach attempts to 'wipe-off' the block towards the team's side so that they can pass, set and spike the wipe-off. The coach then tosses another ball over the net forcing the team to scramble to pass, set and spike. Continue the sequence. One player feeds balls to the coach. The extra players chase balls and feed them to the feeder.

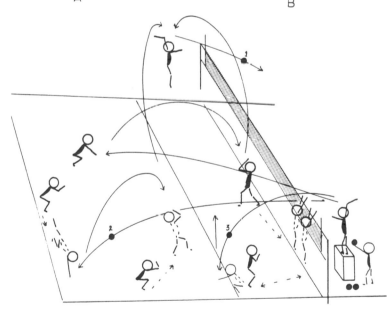

PUT YOUR HEART
INTO THE GAME
AND YOUR BODY WILL
FOLLOW.

OBJECTIVE
To teach total transition

DRILL 399
TRANSITION: TOTAL, 6 PLAYERS, COACH, 10 BALLS, NET

In groups of three. Three players start as blockers and three players start as attackers. The coach tosses the ball to one of the attackers to set to either of the other two attackers. The blockers attempt to block or dig to keep the ball in play. The attackers attempt to do the same with both sides passing, setting and hitting until the ball is dead. Once the ball is dead, the coach throws a second ball to either side to set and hit. If more than two groups are used, rotate in at regular intervals.

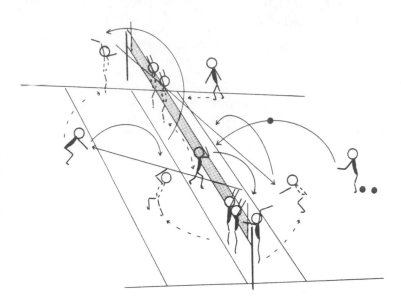

DRILL 400
TRANSITION: TOTAL, 8 PLAYERS, 20 BALLS, NET

Three front-row players and a tosser on each side of the net. (A) One tosser throws a ball up for a front-row player to set and another to spike. The opponents block. The players cover and attempt to keep the ball in play. (B) As soon as the ball is dead, the tosser on the other side of the last team to block throws a new ball over the net for the blockers to pass, set and spike. The extra players chase balls and feed them to the tossers.

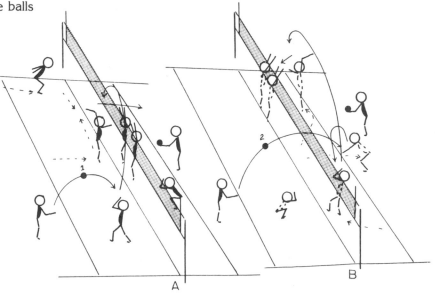

NOTES

NOTES

NOTES

Other Publications by Bob Bratton

300 Plus Drills & Ideas

More than 300 diagrams on drills and tips for coaching volleyball. Drills in this book vary from the author's latest book 400 Plus.

Basic Skills and Concepts

An analysis of the basic skills and step-by-step progressions for teaching the skills.

Team Tactics *+ training $9.50 + $2.50*

This well diagrammed text aimed towards high school coaches and university level volleyball courses is an excellent sequel to "Basic Skills and Concepts".

For further information on Bob Bratton's books and other volleyball publications write to:

Canadian Volleyball Association
1600 James Naismith Drive, Gloucester, Ontario
Canada K1B 5N4